INVESTOR READY

THE GUIDE FOR START-UPS ON GETTING INVESTORS TO SAY *YES*

JULIE BARBER

R3THINK PRESS

First published in Great Britain in 2020 by
Rethink Press (www.rethinkpress.com)

© Copyright Julie Barber

Contents

Introduction

There were sixty people waiting to discover new opportunities as the first start-up founder took to the stage. What followed was a succession of start-ups who didn't understand the market they were pitching to, poorly put-together slide decks and presentations that weren't tailored to the time limit, so essential information was skipped.

It wasn't just the pitch that was the problem; it was clear there were issues with how the start-ups were structured. Scalability and compliance were glaring in their absence. Out of more than ten presentations, only a couple came anywhere near the mark – and after the first five or six, people started to leave. A roomful of potential, wasted.

After a career focused around corporate transformation and innovation, which included extracting over £20 million in business investment from corporate boards, I realised this was my trigger to begin working directly with start-ups and scale-ups. It's a problem I'd repeatedly seen through my corporate innovation work, where I would meet start-up founders for procurement or investment discussions, but the sheer scale of the wasted opportunity I've described above shocked me. And it wasn't a one-off – start-ups and scale-ups are losing potential investors every day because they just aren't *Investor Ready*.

Many start-up founders see raising investment as their route to success, but the investment hurdle is one that they struggle to negotiate. And when it comes down to it, this is hardly surprising: founders start a company because they're really passionate about solving a problem or creating a fun new way of doing something, which means their skills and experience aren't focused on funding rounds.

Getting people to invest in a company requires specific knowledge and skills, which unfortunately aren't taught at school. It's critical not just to present a company and product well, but also to demonstrate that the company itself is strong and running well under the hood. Approaching the investment process without the correct knowledge and skills is a big risk – burning bridges with potential investors is an expensive mistake to avoid at all costs.

Investors may not buy your product, but they are your *other customer*. Their reason to invest will be different from that of a general customer, and they will also have a set of reasons not to invest, which are equally important. Understanding your other customer in depth can mean the difference between success and failure for your company.

Whether your business is a start-up, scale-up or small and medium-sized enterprise (SME), this book will dramatically increase your chances of winning investment by revealing what investors are looking for and what has driven success for the start-ups that have gone before you. Being investor ready doesn't just mean having a great idea, it also means you have a great business. Once you understand this, you can make good choices about the best approach for your company and how to present it to potential investors.

Investor Ready will give you a real understanding of the world of investment and the financing options open to you. It explains the things you need to think about before you start and walks you through the six key principles behind the Investor Ready Roadmap – the process to get companies investor ready. It will take you through what happens after you've secured an investor, giving you a complete handhold from start to finish. Finally, it will share insights from investors, start-up founders and experts from across the ecosystem.

All that remains here is for me to wish you luck on your investment journey – luck that you can create for yourself by being investor ready.

PART ONE

AN OVERVIEW OF INVESTMENT

ONE

Before You Start

Before you dive into planning your investment approach, there are some important things to think about. In this chapter, we'll cover:

- Whether you really need investment

- The importance of preparation

- Your availability to run a raise

- The advice that's worth paying for

- It takes money to raise money

- The long-term impact on your business

Do you really need investment?

You may well reply, 'Of course I do, that's why I'm reading this book', but it's worth challenging yourself on this one. Investment isn't an easy path – it brings with it a host of costs and impacts for your company, as well as potential personal impacts on you as founder.

Raising money gets easier the more traction you have – and that requires a strong product or service backed up by social proof and/or paying customers. A common mistake I see among start-ups is that the founder tries to build the company too big, too early, and consequently they assume they need lots of money. If you engage with your customers and understand what would be a minimum viable product (MVP) for *them* (the smallest version of what you want to create that they would pay for), you can build the MVP at a low cost and start generating revenue while you improve and expand your product.

This applies whether you run a tech company developing an app or a drinks company that wants to launch a new range. The tech company only needs to build an app that is usable, not one that is perfect. The drinks company needs to create one drink, not the whole range, to get it off the ground. If you can keep the costs low, you may be able to leverage your own savings or money from friends and family to help you get to a stage where either you're generating profit and can bootstrap, or you have a much more compelling case for investment.

Whether you need investment is also massively dependent on your ambition and your business model – a multi-continent rollout with asset purchases thrown in, like Uber, isn't going to happen without serious investment. On the other hand, a simple but clever bit of tech that can support customers from an early stage is possible with bootstrapping. You need to balance your ambitions and their costs – see Chapter 5: 'Vision' for help on this.

If you have already got customers, it's about understanding why you need money to get more. If you need a massive capital injection to make your product scalable, then investment makes absolute sense. If your product works fine as it is, and you just need to generate more sales, a grant or a loan to help you hire an amazing salesperson who immediately pays back their worth could be a better way to go.

Nic Brisbourne, Managing Partner at Forward Partners, an early-stage venture capital fund (VC) and start-up studio, explains what directions he might take and why:

> 'It's all about the scale of your ambition and how much capital you need to get there. Capital investment only makes sense for the small percentage of businesses that need

capital to fuel rapid growth. Start-ups that fall into this bracket have a need or desire to outpace the competition and take the market. If this isn't your situation, then you're probably better off bootstrapping.'

Some founders hate the thought of 'giving away' equity and want total control. Shaun Hyland, from Reach Commercial Finance, has experience of founders not taking investment when they should have:

'Owning 100% of a business worth £1 million is probably not quite as good as owning 50% of one that's worth £100 million. A good equity investor often – pretty much always – brings a lot more to the table than just money. A lender brings money and that's it.

'If a lot of founders that I see had taken equity investment when they could have done, it would have accelerated the development of their business and made them prime movers in a fledgling industry. Many people just go for the slow and steady approach which a lender provides, and as a result, they miss the boat.'

The critical question is whether investment is the right route for your business at this time. As Nic identifies, if you do take investment, make sure it's the right kind of investment to match your company's goals.

We'll look more at the different types of investment available in the next chapter.

The importance of preparation

Whatever your investment route, I cannot emphasise enough the importance of good preparation. When my company Spark! works with start-ups and scale-ups, my team and I follow a six- to eight-week timescale for preparation, and that's far from a relaxed pace. Investors have a host of expectations, so putting in the groundwork up front will ultimately drive the success of your investment approach. Good preparation shows professionalism and can reduce the timeline by preventing scrambles later on to get information together. It also minimises the risk of a deal going south when something isn't available. Most importantly, it will reduce your stress levels.

Luke Lang, Co-Founder of Crowdcube, the UK's largest crowdfunding platform, is emphatic on the importance of preparation going into the raise:

> 'This is where the campaign is won and lost.
> The crucial parts of a raise are making sure
> that your comms plan (a communication
> plan is a policy-driven approach to provid-
> ing stakeholders with information)[1] is well
> thought-through and executed, and that

---

1   Definition from www.whatis.com

you've segmented the audiences you feel may
have a high propensity to become shareholders. Planning all of that – thinking about your
messaging, how you're going to position
this investment opportunity to people, and
warming up your community and your existing customer base before a raise goes live – is
increasingly important.'

The story is no different if you're applying for debt
investment. You must be well prepared to make it
easy for the lending institution to say yes to you.

Russell Fisher, Head of Ventures at Nationwide
Building Society, feels start-ups really need to think
ahead:

'If we are getting investor ready, what does the
cap table[2] look like and how quickly could we
get all these guys together if everybody has to
sign on? Have we got the right legal partner
and are they going to be the one to help us do
a deal? That sort of thought tends to get forgot-
ten until the end, and then it can become a bit
fractious.'

There are two times when you shouldn't try to raise
money for your company – too soon and too late.

---

2   'A capitalisation table is a spreadsheet or table that shows the equity
    capitalisation for a company. In general, [it] is an intricate break-
    down of a company's shareholders' equity.' www.investopedia.com/
    terms/c/capitalization-table.asp

That's somewhat flippant, you may say, but if you kick start the process before you're properly ready, you will end up tripping yourself up and potentially burning bridges with investors. Equally, raising investment too late is a bad plan.

I get so many start-up founders coming to me, asking for help with a raise and revealing that their remaining runway (how long their money will last) is only eight to ten weeks, sometimes less time. That gives them no time to prepare well. Never try to raise investment when you're desperate – you may end up agreeing to terms that will be damaging later, simply because you had no other option.

We'll cover the investment process in more detail in Chapter 4 to help you plan how much time you need to allow.

Your availability to run a raise

Any start-up or scale-up founder is likely to tell you they work all the hours under the sun – and that's just on running the company. Raising investment can take a *lot* of time, and understanding the impact that can have is critical.

Deborah Lygonis, Founder of Friendbase, an online world game aimed at teenagers, shared her frustration on the time it takes:

'I feel that I've spent so much time trying to raise money, I'm neglecting the actual business, so that part is really frustrating. I know it's nothing unique, but I sometimes feel like a broken record when I'm sitting at meetings while I could be spending my time doing something so much more productive. It's one of those things you just have to get through, but it's extremely time consuming. A lot of people when they start raising funds don't realise how much time they actually have to spend on it.'

Heather McDonald, Founder and Chief Executive Officer (CEO) of WooHa Brewing Company, recommends delegating what you can to free up your time:

'There's nothing that can prepare you for your first raise. I think most entrepreneurs when they're starting out think that they have the most fantastic idea and the answers to all of the questions, so what could possibly go wrong? What have they not planned for?

'When you do your first raise, even if you have a fantastic idea and plan, it's a lot of hard work to actually convey that to people. They don't necessarily understand where you're coming from or your motivations. The first thing you learn when you do a raise is how hard it is. It's a twenty-four-hour job, and you need to be switched on and concentrating, so offload as much non-raise work as possible to ensure you're not distracted from it.'

It isn't just about making time for the raise, though, as Jonathan Lerner, Managing Director of Smedvig Capital, explains:

'Fundraising is a very time-consuming process. You have to have the time for it. You can't let the wheels fall off the bus, so the business has to be able to trade effectively without your full-time input. Don't miss your numbers during the process. That's really important.'

The ideal situation is to have a co-founder so one of you can run the business and the other can run the raise. If you don't have that option, or you don't yet have staff you can delegate to, you're going to need to make some tough decisions about what is a must have and what's just a nice to have in the business while the raise is happening.

The advice that's worth paying for

Particularly in the early days, when money is tight, you may be tempted to shy away from professional services and do as much as you can yourself. The reality is that people are specialists for a reason – you can't know their area of expertise in the same detail they do, and this is where you can come unstuck. Mistakes you make now may prevent the raise from completing or have long-lasting impacts for your company.

A common area that people cut back on is legal expenses, an approach that worries Russell Fisher:

> 'At Nationwide, we always prefer it when the start-up founder has legal representation, as much to protect them as to protect us. But it can be expensive. What we're finding is we are often the first corporate venture capitalist (CVC) to have engaged with the start-up, and they may feel, "Oh God, they're putting the lawyers on us." We've engaged lawyers because we have to, but the founder is at the stage where they should probably have lawyers involved as well.

> 'Don't think because you've read a book on it or you've googled it, that qualifies you to do the legal side of things, because if you get the agreement wrong with a partner who wants to take advantage, you'll get into all sorts of trouble.'

With legal advice, it's also important not to leave it until the back end of the process. For a start, you need a non-disclosure agreement set up before you share confidential company data with would-be investors.

Elle Berrett, a solicitor from Fusion Law who specialises in working with start-ups, says early is always better for the client:

> 'My colleagues and I always prefer it if a client comes to us at the beginning of the process so that we can get a full picture of exactly what they're trying to achieve and help them achieve that. From our point of view, it's good if they come to us before any documentation has been prepared.'

Companies like SeedLegals are now offering simplified services with key legal forms on their sites that you can pre-fill and lawyers available on instant chat to help with queries, so the legal process doesn't have to be onerous.

Depending on the type and complexity of the raise you're doing, it may be prudent to spend some money on a part-time finance director to support you through the raise process, or a marketing or PR agency. Likewise, if you're completely new to the world of raising investment, then you may want someone to guide you through the process, as my team at Spark! does for start-ups.

Rick Rowan, Founder of NuroKor BioElectronics, wished that he'd had more of a handhold through the process:

'It's like starting a new school or a new job in a new industry where you've never worked before. You've got transferable skills, for example selling and a scientific mindset for the development side of it, but the capital fund-raising side is completely different. Maybe it should be related to what you do, but it's not. It's like a completely different street over here.

'My advice would be for start-ups to get help to go through that process. If I had my time again, I would do it very differently. Hopefully in a less stressful way.'

It takes money to raise money

I frequently meet with early-stage start-up founders who are down to the wire on their budget and trying to raise investment on a shoestring. Not budgeting for the costs of raising investment is a dangerous way to proceed.

As well as the specialist advice we've just covered, you need to think about travel costs, design and print costs, and potentially advertising costs if you're planning on boosting promotional material on social media. Cost and budget for everything. Some services you can pay for post-raise, like your legal advice, but beware! If the deal falls through, you'll still have to pay for any work done up to that point.

The long-term impact on your business

One last thing to consider before you step into raising investment is what it will mean down the road for your company, and for you as founder and CEO. Investment usually brings with it a level of oversight, including board members. Their expertise can obviously be beneficial, but it can create a pressure-cooker environment where you as CEO really start to feel the weight of investors' expectations.

It also means additional time and admin overheads – board reports, shareholder reports and, of course, board meetings. Board meetings themselves aren't a negative – by their nature, they're an asset to a company – but be aware of the time they'll take up and how your role needs to change to accommodate them.

Then there's a slightly less pleasant potential impact for founders. If investors hold a significant enough stake, they can at some point in the future make a decision to remove you as CEO and bring in someone more experienced to take the company through the next stages of its life.

It isn't all doom and gloom, though. Apart from getting the money, there's another great upside to raising investment. Companies that are under the 'investment microscope' are usually stronger. They do things properly and have better plans for the future.

You should now have a good idea of some of the key impacts of raising investment, both during the exercise and afterwards. If you only take away one thing from this chapter, make it a knowledge of how much forward thinking and planning you need to do to make your raise a success.

Before you progress on to the next chapter, I recommend you visit the 'Are You Investor Ready?' tool at www.spark-consulting.co.uk/are-you-investor-ready. It's a free fifty-question review that will act as a great benchmark for you. You'll get a report emailed to you of your answers so you can see where you have gaps. You can then use this report alongside the book to help you become fully investor ready.

TWO

What Type Of Finance Is Right For You?

There's more than one way to raise money for your company. In this chapter, we'll cover:

- The raise stages
- The four types of investment
- The debt spectrum
- Choosing the right route

The raise stages

You're likely to hear lots of terms bandied around about the different levels of raise that exist. Here, I'll give you my definitions, as well as sharing what some investors think.

Pre-seed

This is the earliest round of funding you can do. Typically, the company has a small team at this point, often the founders only, and no product or revenue yet. The raise you'll do here funds product build or asset acquisition. It can be any amount from £30k–£250k.

Seed

At seed, you'll probably have a small team and a product that people can use. The product needs to either be generating revenue or have good customer traction that will turn into revenue later on (think of an app that launches on a free basis, and then adds premium paid-for offerings later). Seed raises are usually in the £250k–£2 million range.

Russell Fisher shares his expectations of a seed-stage company:

> 'For me, seed means there's proof of life, there's traction, there are customers paying for something or engaging with it. That's what I want to see. And I want to see growth stories, I want to see positive net promoter score (NPS).'

Series A

According to CB Insights, only 48% of companies that raised seed funding make it as far as a series A raise.[3] Many companies never make it this far because either they can bootstrap from seed or the company has folded. Series A requires serious commercial traction and the signs of a great company in the making, with raises ranging from £2–10 million.

Series B

We're firmly into scale-up territory now. Series B companies have clear product/market fit (more on that in Chapter 8) and need to fund customer acquisition and business scaling. They might be raising anywhere from £7–15 million.

After series B, the raises can keep coming, all the way up to series G in some cases, before the company moves to initial public offering (IPO). But the funnel gets smaller on the way up, with more and more companies dropping out at each level.

Not every company progresses up the raise ladder – you'll need to make a choice, depending on your company's circumstances, whether you keep raising the next round, and the next. Just because you do one raise doesn't mean you need to do another. If one raise

---

3   www.cbinsights.com/research/venture-capital-funnel-2

gets you over the hump and into a position where you have a workable product and customer traction, then your own profits may be enough to drive you forward from there.

Building a high-growth company with a massive valuation doesn't have to mean raising rounds at all. There are plenty of companies that have bootstrapped their way to the top, ie grown by investing profits back into the business. Plenty of companies take alternative routes as well.

Chris Adelsbach, Angel Investor of the Year and Techstars Venture Partner, was previously a founder who grew his business to a $500 million exit with only one round of equity investment:

> 'We didn't take any angel or VC money; we used our own money, and then took one round of private equity. After that, we used balance sheet leverage. There were fewer options in 2009, though, so I may have made a different choice today.'

That said, many early-stage VC funds act as feeders into later Stage Ones, so if you do think you'll need multiple raises, it's worth getting on the ladder early. Jonathan Lerner, Managing Director at Smedvig Capital, explains:

'We get a lot of our deal flow from people who fundraised earlier with other funds. As a result, we know all the earliest stage funds really well and spend a lot of time going through their portfolios and understanding where businesses are going, which ones are coming up for funding, and then working out which ones fit with our criteria, which ones don't.'

The four types of investment

It's a common misconception that equity investment is the only growth route available to start-ups. This is because equity investment is in the news and widely discussed across start-up communities. 'Raising a round' is in danger of becoming a standard path, when it's probably not suitable for many companies.

There are actually four main types of investment open to any business: grants, reward-based funding, equity and debt. The important bit is working out which one is right for you.

Grants

Business grants are available from a number of government organisations and charitable trusts set up to support business growth. Unlike debt or equity providers, these organisations aren't expecting repayment of funds or a cash return on investment (ROI); they're often focused on other economic measures instead, such as generating employment and keeping the UK at the forefront of technological advances.

Vanessa Tierney, Co-Founder and CEO of Abodoo, a smart-working talent platform, explains her experience of raising grant funding:

> 'Due diligence for government funding is stringent and your strategy needs to be prudent. Your forecasting needs to be *very* prudent. Whereas VCs and angel investors want to see big and bold vision, governments want to see something you'll easily and comfortably achieve, because their focus is not ROI, it's employees. How many people are you going to employ in the next two to three years? Governments put money into start-ups in the hope of creating new employment opportunities. And the focus is on who you'll take on, so it's not a case of saying, "I'll hire five people." You need to have identified the talent that you have now and who you will need. It's all about being reassuring.'

Apart from the stringent due diligence, there are three other challenges to be aware of with grants:

- There are absolutely *loads* of different grants out there, and sifting through which ones you may be eligible for takes up valuable time.

- Once you've found which ones you want, actually applying for them also takes a huge amount of time.

- Government grants often 'match fund', which means they'll put up a certain amount of money as long as you do too. This is not great if you don't have sufficient funds and can mean you still need to raise other investment as well.

You can spend a few hours on Google, talk to your local council's business advice support services, or even hire a company to find and apply for the right grants for you. Be aware with this last option that the company will get a percentage of the grant.

Reward-based funding

This is generally used at pre-seed, ie to fund product development. Fairly small amounts of money are raised, through crowdfunding platforms that offer a reward-based option. Instead of getting equity in return for cash, investors donate cash to get a chance to use the product in the future, or get some kind of gift associated with the product.

David Horne, Founder of Add Then Multiply and a portfolio chief finance officer (CFO), explains how reward-based funding worked for one of his ventures:

> 'One of the first start-ups I co-founded was an online TV platform that had a very specific targeted niche customer. The founder, a BBC trained television producer, was reasonably well known, so he had credibility. We shot a professional video, put it out on to social media, and said, "Here's what we're going to do. Here's what we plan to do. Here are some of the programmes we're looking at, and here's how the thing is going to work. We are looking for people to be founder subscribers, and in return for £100, you'll get a two-year subscription."

> 'We went out through social media to our niche marketplace and raised £50,000. That enabled us to get the first batch of stuff off the ground, get a working prototype of what the thing was going to look like and get some content.'

Reward-based funding suits start-up founders with a simple and easily explainable product who don't qualify for a business loan and have insufficient product and/or traction to attract equity investment. It can be a great way of building crowd awareness of the product in the early stages, although you do need to be careful how much you divulge, and protect yourself with patents and trademarks wherever possible in advance. At such an early stage, it's easy for someone else to steal your idea and speed past you.

On the plus side, the costs to get a campaign up and running are fairly low, although you'll still need to sort some things out, like a video and a basic deck (if you're unfamiliar with the term 'deck' in this context, we will cover it in detail in Chapter 11). Things to watch out for are how much of the raise amount the platform will take as commission – this can be anywhere between 5–13% (or up to 40% in the United States), so you need to factor that into your budget. Also, if you don't raise the full amount you're seeking, you may forfeit all the money, so read the raise terms carefully.

Equity

Equity investment is basically an exchange of value – money for equity in your company, ie a percentage of the total shareholding. Equity investors are looking for a sizeable ROI (anywhere from 4–10x as a basic expectation, with the hope in the back of their minds that it might soar to 100x). Typically, they expect to get that return through an exit at some point in the future, where the whole company is sold to another larger entity at a much higher price than when they originally invested, or through an IPO where the company is floated on the stock market.

According to CB Insights, nearly 67% of start-ups fail to reach an exit or raise follow-on funding,[4] so equity investment is a high-risk gamble for investors. You can buy back shares from investors, but they will still expect to see an appropriate ROI in the price they are paid – an option many companies can't afford without an exit. We'll explore the different types of people and organisations who invest in equity in Chapter 10, 'Investors'.

Another option is convertible debt – a kind of half-way house between debt and equity. Here, investors make a loan to the start-up under specific terms that allow them the option to convert what they are owed into equity at a later date. There is usually an incentive for them to convert to equity in the form of a discount or a warrant.

Until the investors convert to equity, you may have to make repayments against the loan amount at an agreed interest rate. This can be useful if you believe your valuation will soar quickly so you don't want to sell equity too cheaply now, or if it's too early to reliably value your start-up at all.

Equity investment is good for start-ups that:

• Have a long runway to profit and will need capital to sustain them until they break even

---

4   www.cbinsights.com/research/venture-capital-funnel-2

- Have huge growth plans

- Need large amounts of capital early to finance asset acquisition (think starting an airline or a limousine service)

Debt

Not all start-ups can access debt – it's dependent on traction and the type of company. Cryptocurrency start-ups, for example, often struggle to even get a bank account, let alone debt, due to concerns about money laundering.

Banks can be slow to respond and their business advisors are usually people who've never run a business and/or don't understand the cutting edge technologies that many start-ups are developing, so convincing them you're a good bet can be a tall order. To qualify for debt, you need to be generating revenue that you can make repayments from.

Debt can be a great option if:

- You have a short-term capital need (the nasty gap between being able to take on big contracts and having enough people/product to actually fulfil them)

- You don't need massive amounts of money

- You don't have the runway left to go through a full equity raise – you can actually use debt to extend your runway and give you time to raise equity properly

Debt is usually on a pure repayment basis at a set interest rate, although in the United States some companies are starting to offer debt in return for a percentage of revenue. This new model isn't prevalent in the UK at the time of writing.

The debt spectrum

There is a wide spectrum of debt options available, dependent on the business circumstances and the cost of borrowing that the company can afford.

Standard business loans

Within the standard business loan arena, there are generally four types of lending:

High street banks are the ultimate option – the Holy Grail, if you like – of business lending, partly because if you have a business bank account, you'll already have a relationship with them, and partly because of the rates they can offer.

Shaun Hyland from Reach Commercial Finance explains:

'Part of the reason why banks are the best places to be is that they've got the lowest cost of funds. To a large extent, they're paying deposit account people half a per cent or less for their money – that's their cost of funds – so they should be able to pass that on in the form of lower pricing in terms of debt.'

If you don't quite have the security needed to get a bank loan under normal criteria, you can enquire about a loan under the protection of the Enterprise Finance Guarantee. Backed by the UK government, this gives lenders a 75% guarantee against the outstanding loan balance, and has so far enabled more than 40,000 businesses to get loans they wouldn't otherwise have qualified for.

Where your company doesn't meet the standard business loan criteria for a high street bank, you still have two other options: specialist lenders and what I term 'money+ lenders'.

Specialist lenders are generally accessible via a broker and will deal with trickier loan circumstances, for example business types that perhaps banks wouldn't touch, but they are usually more expensive because the risk profile is higher and their cost of finance is also higher. They don't have access to the deposit funds that banks do, so they have to buy their debt financing in at a premium.

There are specific SME debt funds that manage European, UK, regional or London government money to provide loans to businesses that wouldn't otherwise qualify. The FSE Group manages a number of these funds and offers loans from £100k to £1 million over periods of up to five years.

Money+ lenders are institutions that market specifically to start-ups and offer not just a loan, but also additional help such as mentoring and writing business plans. The UK government offers start-up business loans of this type, as does Virgin StartUp, both in the £500 to £25k range. They're usually a personal loan, not a business loan, so there is risk to your personal assets if you default on repayments.

Peer-to-peer lending

Peer-to-peer lending is a fairly new approach – crowd-funding from a different angle, where people can make their money available to lend to others through a centralised platform. Leaders in the space are Funding Circle, LendingClub, Upstart and Fundrise. They pride themselves on speedy turnarounds, and from initial contact to money in the bank can be as little as five days.

You usually apply online, but then have to provide follow-up documentation and answer further questions from these lenders' debt assessors. As with banks, you'll need to provide your most recent statutory year-end accounts, including a detailed profit-loss and current year management accounts. They will also usually request six months' worth of bank statements, which must include all your business bank accounts, any deposit accounts and your last five VAT returns.

This type of debt almost always includes a personal guarantee, so you need to be aware of what that means going in. Your house, your car and your pension could be on the line.

Invoice discounting

Invoice discounting is a type of short-term finance that allows you to get money for invoices you have issued before your client actually pays them. The providers who offer this take on the whole of the invoice as debt and pay you a percentage of the amount you're owed immediately as cash. Then when you get paid by the client, you pay the provider the whole invoice amount, so they make their money on the difference between what you pay them and what they gave you.

You can do block discounting on a regular basis or use this on one-off invoices, so it can be really useful for short-term cash-flow issues, but it isn't going to provide massive growth potential. Ultimately, you're losing revenue and profits, so it certainly shouldn't be a long-term strategy.

It also doesn't work for every type of business, as Shaun Hyland explains:

'If you're in retail, it doesn't work at all because there are no debtors. And in some industries, the nature of the debts created is not suitable for discounting. Probably the best example is the construction industry, along with software, tech businesses and others where there is an ongoing commitment to the client. These become difficult to fund with invoice discounting because there's no clear point at which the clients' needs are reaching fulfilment.

'For example, if you have a two-year service agreement for a tech business, and you are billing monthly in advance, then you would only be able to discount that debt when you've delivered the service. So despite the fact that you invoice the customer on the first of the month for the current month, you wouldn't be able to discount the invoice until the last day of the month. But if you're on thirty-day terms, you've already been paid anyway, so what would be the point in discounting?'

Factoring

Factoring is similar to invoice discounting, but here the lender takes on full credit control of the debt. This is tricky if you're in a relationship business – you're not likely to want a debt provider contacting your clients, asking when they'll be paying their invoice.

R&D tax credits financing

With the huge number of tech start-ups around, research and development (R&D) tax credits have never been so relevant. Particularly useful if your company needs a single cash boost to get it past a particular hurdle, this type of financing allows you to borrow against R&D tax credits claims up to six months in advance. And you'll be able to borrow against a greater percentage of the claim if you have prior history of claims going through successfully. Companies like GrantTree take a dual approach here, preparing the R&D tax claim for you as well as arranging the finance against it.

Choosing the right route

Choosing the right investment route for your company is a balancing act. It's all about working out:

- Which type of investor you'll be more attractive to

- Which type of investor can provide the level of finance you need

- What kind of terms you're looking for

- What length of time you have before you need the money

- How long you need the money for

- Whether you can start making repayments right away

Taking one route to start with doesn't mean you're always bound to follow that route. Some start-ups may begin with a business loan from the government, then do some reward-based funding to help build their MVP, and then go on to debt funding or equity raises as they continue to scale. Assessing what is right for your company now and in the future is critical.

Here's a quick summary of the pros and cons of each route:

Type of investment	Pros	Cons
Grants	• You don't need to pay the money back • Winning a grant can add credibility to later funding rounds	• Finding the right fund takes a big time investment • Competition for some grants is fierce • Many grants only do match-funding
Reward-based Funding	• You don't need to pay the money back	• Only works for small amounts of money • High % charges from platforms in many cases
Debt	• Quicker to access in most cases • Great for covering short-term cash gaps	• Often only available to later-stage companies that can prove they can repay • Cost of borrowing can be high
Equity	• Can raise large amounts of money • Money often comes with additional expertise	• Reduces your equity holding • Added pressure of investors • Often long timescale to win and access investment

Now you have an understanding of the different investment routes, let's look in detail at the world of equity.

THREE

The Equity Investment Landscape

The world of equity is huge, complex and ever-changing. It's a good idea to be aware of how you fit into the ecosystem, so in this chapter we'll take a look at:

- How much money is available

- Emerging trends

- Equality in investment

How much money is available

If you ask how much money is out there for start-up and scale-up funding, the answer is a lot. According to projections by Crunchbase, over $1.5 trillion in VC deals were done worldwide from 2010–2019, with roughly $295 billion of that in 2019 alone, covering everything from pre-seed to pre-IPO rounds.[5] The year 2019 saw a bit of a dip in dollar volume from 2018, but overall it's been a substantial upward trend since 2012. Deal volume continued to climb with a record-breaking high in the third quarter of 2019, which levelled out to a small rise in 2019 overall.

Globally, the large majority of investment goes at seed level, although PitchBook's 2019 Annual European Venture Report suggests a reduction in European seed and early-stage funding with more emphasis in later stages.[6] Between January 2016–2019, over 50% of seed rounds were crowdfunded, which shows the increasing democratisation of investment, moving it away from the more traditional routes of VC and private equity.

Emerging trends

While fintech continues to dominate, artificial intelligence (AI), healthtech and e-commerce are hot on its heels in terms of investment dollars. Healthtech is an area that is only going to get hotter, with increased interest around digital therapeutics and healthy habits, not to mention the mental health cause. The other

---

5   https://news.crunchbase.com/news/the-q4-eoy-2019-global-vc-report-a-strong-end-to-a-good-but-not-fantastic-year
6   https://pitchbook.com/news/reports/2019-annual-european-venture-report

emerging sectors are cleantech and transport, with their potential positive impact on climate change. All electric forms of transport are drawing attention.

Across all the investment sectors, there is a powerful sentiment rising, as Luke Lang explains:

'Particularly in the last two, three years, there's been a definite shift of emphasis towards mission. And I think that's partly driven by the entrepreneurs of today: our Millennials, Generations X and Z, who are starting businesses because they want to make a difference. They want a purpose behind what they're doing, in the same way that consumers are becoming more considered and conscious of the businesses and brands that they purchase from. We're starting to see this next generation of entrepreneur take flight.

'Tom at Monzo is a great example of that. He didn't just want to start a new bank in the same guise as the old bank; he wanted to start a completely new bank and do it differently, transform things and do it in a more open, inclusive way. We're seeing the best businesses understand the need to tell a story. There's a new wave of entrepreneurs that are living on that, and that's why they're getting into business and starting companies.

'And that's beautifully supported by customers and consumers who increasingly want businesses that stand for something, that are trying to make a difference. It's a belief economy, where we've got businesses with a deep sense of purpose and a set of values and beliefs that they adhere to. We've got consumers that really buy into this and want to be part of it and get involved in those businesses because they genuinely believe in them.'

There is also change coming in the timeframes for raises. In a traditional raise cycle, businesses would seek investment every eighteen to twenty-four months, but with the use of technology, the rate of growth now possible is such that many unicorns (companies valued at $1billion+) are finding themselves raising every six or seven months, just to keep pace. For smaller start-ups with the same challenges, companies like SeedLegals are offering simple advanced subscription agreements and convertible loan notes that allow them to raise outside of a round, which reduces cost and effort.

When it comes to raising funding, the process can be painful and slow. Companies like Swoop are trying to address this by offering access to grants, loans and equity via an app, using banking data as the main qualifier.

Bigger exits and investor returns are also an increasing trend. Nic Brisbourne thinks this can force companies into plans that aren't right for them:

> 'One of the trends that has been playing out over the last few years is that VCs are increasingly targeting bigger and bigger returns. You've got to be talking 10x, not 3x. This means there are a lot of businesses with exit potential in the mid-hundreds of millions that are either struggling to get financing or re-cutting their plans to target a billion plus exit. This may not be where they naturally fit.'

Interestingly, the rise of so many new businesses is leading to opinion that more should be done to teach entrepreneurial skills to children and young adults, to equip them better for running their own companies. Ed Stephens, Head of Brokerage at the Angel Investment Network, explains why he feels it's important:

> 'We really care about supporting entrepreneurship. This starts with education so that the aggregate level of entrepreneurship improves. In my experience of teaching, there are some kids who are brilliant at computer science, but aren't being given the tools they need to know how to value a business, raise money for it or even incorporate a company. These skills are essential, so we want to make kids who are

entrepreneurial aware of their choices and the reality of how they realise them.

'Innovation and entrepreneurship will be essential to how we continue to grow our economy, so entrepreneurs should be competent in all the necessary skills to develop a company without having to lean on investors' capital. It shouldn't be that we have to tell people that a fundraising deck looks like this or financials are presented like that. That's lost time.'

Ed's view is echoed in the Rose Review, which we'll cover in more detail later in the chapter. Some educational establishments, such as Aston Business School, are offering MScs in entrepreneurship, but there is more to be done at the earlier stages of education, particularly to reach those who may never take a degree.

Equality in investment

Equality in investment, both in who invests and who is funded, has been a hot topic in recent years. Historically, the world of equity investment has been about as lacking in diversity as you can get, but pressure from institutional investors and new approaches to investment are helping to turn the tide.

The sixth edition of KPMG's Women in Alternative Investments (WAI) Report, *The Call To Act*, revealed

75% of investors in hedge fund, private equity and property firms said they would challenge those firms on their gender diversity in the next year, with 42% requiring an active improvement.[7] VC firms emerged as the most progressive, with 27% having a female chief executive or chief investment officer, but equality falls off a cliff in mainstream private equity with only a 7% female representation.

There's also a new trend around equality investing with companies like Mirova launching equity funds focusing on companies that promote gender equality and women's representation in top-level management. But although the tide is turning, in some cases it's more of a trickle than a tidal wave. The United States made the headlines in December 2019 because investment in female founders hit an all-time high – yes, a whopping 2.8% of all equity!

There was good news in the Crunchbase End of Year Diversity Report for 2019, which revealed 20% of global start-ups raising their first round had a female founder – a 100% increase since 2010.[8] In addition, since 2014, more than 10,000 start-ups with at least one female founder have successfully completed a raise, and fifteen female-founded start-ups became unicorns. On the flip side, 87% of the dollar volume is still going to male-only start-ups via 81% of the deals,

7   https://assets.kpmg/content/dam/kpmg/us/pdf/2019/02/
     women-in-ai-report.pdf
8   https://news.crunchbase.com/news/eoy-2019-diversity-report-
     20-percent-of-newly-funded-startups-in-2019-have-a-female-founder

so men are not only doing more deals, but getting more money per deal as well.

Russell Fisher is keen to redress the balance on diversity as a whole:

> 'The amount of focus given to London is wrong. The amount of focus given to male founders is wrong. There is some awesome stuff going on outside London and there's some awesome stuff going on with female founders. There seems to be a bias, I think because the current investment process favours bravado and bold positioning – typical male stuff like that. When we've found female founders, they tend to be quite understated and talk down their success.'

Vanessa Tierney sees it as a style difference between men and women that can create the barrier:

> 'There is a difference because you're pitching predominantly to men. The reality is within the investment world, there are not many women. If I look at angel investors, if I look at the government grant funding, I would say 80 to 90% [of investors] have been male.

> 'Women tend to present differently to men, and perhaps their confidence or boldness is not as high, so when we're dealing with investors

who are used to getting a certain type of pitch, there's sometimes a mis-marriage. Maybe if there was more of a diverse panel reviewing us, it would help.'

Some female founders, like Deborah Lygonis from Friendbase, have found they've had to change their style to put themselves on an equal footing with men:

'I've been recommended to bring on a male CEO, but we haven't gone down that route yet. Instead, I've changed my own presentation on LinkedIn. I tend to brag a lot about my previous tech investments – I actually *do* work with rocket science, because several of the companies that I coach are in that space. That really isn't who I am, because normally I would never bang my own drum, but in business I find that it's a necessity.'

The biggest thing that has sent shockwaves through the UK investment community is the publication of the Alison Rose Review of Female Entrepreneurship in 2019.[9] A government-sponsored review, it found that closing the gap between female and male entrepreneurs could mean £250 billion in gross value add to the UK economy – the equivalent of four *years'* economic growth.

---

9   www.gov.uk/government/publications/the-alison-rose-review-of-female-entrepreneurship

The review found five key areas that needed work to achieve this – everything from awareness of capital availability to disproportionate primary care responsibilities. Eight initiatives have been identified as a result, including a new Investing in Female Entrepreneurs Code and the roll out of entrepreneurship-related courses in schools and colleges.

Luke Lang feels crowdfunding has driven long-lasting change and more in the investment world for female entrepreneurs:

'We've helped level the playing field for all minority groups, whether that's ethnicity, background, socio-economic or gender. Prior to Crowdcube, I felt the die was cast heavily in favour of male entrepreneurs because the majority of investment came from men, often in their forties and fifties. And whether that's right or wrong, it clearly had an impact on the people that they were backing and investing in.

'What Crowdcube did was remove all of those barriers, break them down, enable good entrepreneurs to access capital from a much broader investor base, which was perhaps more open minded with a lack of preconceptions. This new model increasingly empowered the entrepreneur to leverage their own network.

'If you are a female founder and you've got a great product, and your customer base tends to be dominated by females, that's not a disadvantage with us. You could still get individuals to invest in and back your business. It's about removing a lot of the barriers for all entrepreneurs, not just females, but it seems to have had a more profound effect on female entrepreneurs who have seized upon Crowdcube as a way of raising finance for their business. The more we can do and the more role models we can produce and celebrate to give other females the confidence to start their own business, to be ambitious, to raise growth capital or equity finance, the better it will be for everyone.'

For some founders, being female is a point of difference that they can exploit. Heather McDonald explains her experience:

'For me, being a woman has been beneficial, because a lot of breweries are presented to by guys. Instead, I'm standing there in my heels, so it's something different. It's something they don't normally see, so it probably plays in my favour.'

An equality issue that isn't talked about quite as much is that of underprivileged founders. Investors usually expect founders to have 'skin in the game', ie to have put down some of their own money to help finance the company. They don't count what's called 'sweat equity', (where founders work on the company without getting paid). For founders who can't afford to contribute thousands of their own money, this can make it even harder to get investment. Some angel investors and VCs are starting to fund without requiring founder finance, but they're in the minority.

There are some hot trends in the world of investment. If your start-up fits within one of those trends, it could definitely help your cause. If not, you might need to work a bit harder to grab attention.

Now that you've got a sense of what's going on in the world of equity, it's time to look at the investment process.

FOUR

The Investment Process

From here on in, we'll mainly focus on an equity raise, but the principles and steps are similar no matter what route to investment you choose. In this chapter, we'll cover:

- The four stages of investment
- Introducing the Investor Ready Roadmap

The four stages of investment

It's important to understand the four stages that you'll go through when raising investment, not least because it will help you to plan how much time you need and how to manage your business cash-flow in the meantime. The timeline can stretch in and out massively depending on many different factors – which type of investors you're going for, whether you find the right investor quickly, whether due diligence throws up any tricky questions and even how long it takes to transfer the money once the deal is done.

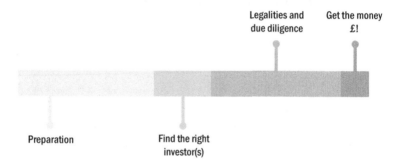

Legalities and
due diligence

Get the money
£!

Preparation

Find the right
investor(s)

One of the worst mistakes I see with founders is that they leave raising too late. I frequently get phone calls revealing they only have eight to ten weeks' runway left. If they can access debt finance, then they might still be able to reach a solution, but trying to raise equity funding within that timeframe is impossible in most cases. This is why you need to have a good grasp on your business, how much money it needs to keep it alive and when it will run out, so you can plan ahead for your next raise effectively.

The four stages of investment are:

Stage One: Preparation

Typically this will take between four to eight weeks to pull together, depending on the size of the organisation and the level of experience of the founders. As we covered in Chapter 1, it's worth spending the time on your preparation as it will not only save you time and stress later, it will make you appear more credible and give you more confidence throughout the process. If your company qualifies, make sure that you apply for Advance Assurance under the Seed Enterprise Investment Scheme (SEIS) or Enterprise Investment Scheme (EIS) during this period as well, as investors will want to know you have this done. We'll cover what this is in more depth in the 'Investors' chapter.

Stage Two: Finding investors

If you've done your prep, you'll have a target list of key investors. This should cut down your time outlay, but you can still expect this part of the process to take anywhere between three to eight weeks. It isn't about just getting a meeting; it's about the internal processes investors follow.

Jonathan Lerner gives some insight into how his company's processes work:

'With Smedvig Capital, there's a clear process. How the investment opportunity comes in is varied – someone might come in to a partner, they might go in to an associate, and then we'll start working out and do what we internally call a 'one-pager'. It's the first time the team talks about it. We'll try to do that within days of it coming in, if we think it's interesting and imminent, so that we can start to get input from the team of what we like, what we don't like about it.

'We work that quickly into a multi-pager – same thing as the one-pager, but much longer and more detailed. Working with the start-up founder at that point is normally a junior and a senior, building an investment case and why they think it's exciting.

'The final stage is the founder coming to present their proposal to our internal investment committee, and then we'll issue a term sheet. Although everyone follows the same process, the speed of the process can vary hugely.'

The 'term sheet' is a document that is used by companies and investors to agree the terms of the deal they are about to do (more on that in Chapter 10). Whoever issues the term sheet will write down the terms they want to do the deal on, and then it's down to the other party to either agree or negotiate for changes. The terms can cover everything from how much money will be invested and the percentage of ownership the investor can expect, to how and when the money will be paid and what other control the investor will have in the business.

Stage Three: Legalities and due diligence

Depending on the investor, the complexity of the company and the level of readiness of the founders, this can take anywhere from one to eight weeks to complete – plenty of time to chew down your nails while you nervously pray that the deal goes through. We'll go through the detail of this stage in Chapter 12.

Stage Four: Getting the money

I used to joke that this is the only stage that doesn't hurt, but unfortunately some start-ups find it can take almost as long as the preparation stage. This can be due to individual angels having to release money before they can provide it, or corporate VCs who are new to the venture world and don't have all their processes running smoothly yet.

What is the Investor Ready Roadmap?

Before we move on to the next chapter, I want to introduce you to the Investor Ready Roadmap, the tool my company Spark! uses to help clients increase their chances of winning investment. It consists of six steps that guide you through Stage One of the investment process: preparation.

By the time you've completed the roadmap steps, you'll be able to see your business through an investor's eyes. You'll understand their worries and what you need to do to assuage those worries, so that they can proceed to a clear yes. You'll also have done all the prep you need to make the first three stages of investment as smooth as possible. It can't help with Stage Four (getting the money), unfortunately!

The six steps of the Investor Ready Roadmap are:

- **Vision.** Finding the right investor and winning them over is only possible if you know what you want for your company in the future. Having clarity on your company vision is the first step on the path to being investor ready.

- **Structure and scale.** A great pitch might get you through the door, but your company has to hold up when an investor lifts the hood and looks into the detail of its setup and its ability to cope with growth.

- **Market.** Being clear on your brand, product/ market fit, defending your market position and creating a go-to-market strategy are all covered by this step.

- **Numbers.** This covers everything from forward projections to valuations and the raise itself.

Getting this step right is critical to pass investor scrutiny.

- **Investors.** Understanding the types of investors there are, getting to grips with SEIS and EIS schemes, and creating a raise strategy all form part of this step.

- **Pitch.** The final step, covering everything you will present to investors – your pitch deck, your business plan, one-pagers, data rooms and product demos.

It's important to follow the steps in order, as each of them draws on the ones before. Are you ready? Enjoy!

PART TWO

THE INVESTOR READY ROADMAP

FIVE

Step One – Vision

This chapter covers two key points:

- What is a business vision?

- Why investors care about vision

What is a business vision?

There are multiple theories about what a business vision is and how it should be constructed. The approach we use at Spark!, which is what we will cover in this chapter, helps to link things together in a way that makes sense for investors.

A business vision is made up of five things:

- Problem

- Mission

- Passion

- Solution

- Ambition

To make it clear how each of these five parts works, I'm going to use the example of a fictional start-up called H_2O with a founder called Miriam.

Problem

The first and key thing every company founder must establish is the problem their company is here to solve. The more specific you can be, the better – investors don't like wishy washy. This isn't your ambition, it's just the problem your business can solve and the impacts it creates.

H_2O'S PROBLEM

The problem our fictional start-up, H_2O, has identified is: 'There is too much plastic in the ocean, which is killing sea life and destroying shoreline habitats, and more is being added all the time.'

Mission

The mission statement is the moon shot, the ultimate goal. Bill Gates and Paul Allen famously had a dream for Microsoft of 'A computer on every desk and in every home', while Elon Musk's mission for Tesla is 'To accelerate the world's transition to sustainable energy'. Your mission doesn't have to be quite that dramatic – it's just as valid to have a mission to create celebration cakes that fill their recipients with joy (and cake).

H_2O'S MISSION

Our imaginary founder, Miriam, has this mission: 'To eradicate 90% of all plastic from the world's oceans by 2030.'

Passion

The passion is a critical part of how you hook investors. Your story, your key motivator is what demonstrates your passion. It tells people who you are at your core and why you're doing what you do. Whether you have a desire to help humankind or a personal reason, like a family member who is affected by something you want to address, being clear on your passion is incredibly powerful.

H$_2$O'S PASSION

Our founder, Miriam, grew up near a beautiful coastline which is now littered with plastic, and the bodies of fish and sea mammals who have choked on the plastic in the water. Her driving passion is to see places like this restored to how they once were. In addition, she is a marine biologist and has seen the same damage everywhere. She views the world as 'choking on plastic'.

Luke Lang thinks passion and purpose are becoming more and more important in how we articulate our vision:

'At Crowdcube, we're increasingly seeing founders who are much better at telling the story of why and how they started the business, the vision that they have for the company, the difference they want to make in the world and the purpose that's driving them. And that can be a really powerful narrative to inspire not just customers, but investors as well.

'That story is often grounded in something personal that plays out of a problem they've tried to solve or an experience they've had where they want to improve something, make something better, whether it's Tom at Monzo, who's transforming personal banking, or Pip from Pip & Nut, who just wants to make healthy, nutritious peanut butter as a result of being unable to find anything suitable to eat while training for a marathon.

'You know what your purpose is, what you believe in and what difference you want to make. I always feel that's the bit that really inspires people. That's the bit that bashes them over the head and captivates them, grabs their attention. And that, in many ways, is sometimes the hardest bit for people to write down in a concise and compelling way.'

Solution

Your solution must solve your problem – sounds simple enough, but you may be surprised by how many business ideas there are where the problem doesn't fit the solution, and vice versa. Then founders end up having to go back to work on both things.

H_2O'S SOLUTION

Miriam knows that the problem – too much plastic in the ocean – needs to have a two-part solution. There needs to be a way to clean up all the plastic currently in the ocean, and a way to stop plastic ending up in the ocean in the first place.

First, a plastic collector can be placed near key ocean currents to trap plastic and allow it to be collected and recycled safely. Second, a consultancy will work with major global corporations on how they can eradicate plastic from their operations – the fees from the consultancy will pay for the ocean clean up exercise and fund exploration of natural material alternatives.

Ambition

Ambition covers what kind of company you need to create to deploy the solution and achieve your mission. Getting the detail of this right allows you to understand what your company needs to look and feel like in eighteen months, three years, five years and ten years' time. You do this on a 'fade' basis – lots of detail for the next three years, less detail for five years, high level for ten years.

H₂O'S AMBITION

Miriam knows that in ten years' time, she wants a global organisation that is efficient at keeping the oceans clean, and has relationships with large- and medium-sized companies across the globe that fund both the continued ocean clean up and the exploration and manufacture of new natural materials to replace plastic. She can't achieve all of that straight away, so in the first three years, the consultancy will be focused on the UK and expansion into France only, with one ocean 'garbage patch' targeted and three particular stretches of UK and French coastline destined for total clean up.

To achieve her ambitions, Miriam will work out what she needs for the company to function at that level.

How many people will she need? What outsourced help (accountants, lawyers, a marketing agency perhaps)? What technology? What's the cost of delivery, etc? She also needs to work out what the obligations are for a company of that size - VAT registration, annual accounts, corporation tax returns, Information Commissioner's Office (ICO) registration, insurance, employee benefits etc - as obligations mean costs. Collectively, this will help Miriam to understand how much it will cost to achieve her mission. This is important data that she will use when she comes to the Numbers step on the Investor Ready Roadmap to calculate forward projections and the amount of money she needs to raise.

Once you've defined the problem your business can solve, been clear about the mission and unearthed why you're passionate about what you do, articulated your solution and outlined your ambition, that collective vision will really help you stay on course whenever you're thinking about what to do next.

Now let's explore...

Why investors care about vision

Journey

Investing in a business essentially means joining the founders on a journey over the next few years, so investors need to be happy with what the destination is going to be and what the potential return is.

Angel investor Chris Adelsbach explains more:

'It's helpful for start-up founders to paint a grand picture of where they want to take the business, because no early investor will invest to double or triple their money; they invest to make 50–100x their money. I want to understand how ambitious the founder really is.

'With that said, I do not want them to paint such a broad vision that they don't concentrate on a specific-use case, a specific vertical. I am looking for somebody who paints a picture of where their business could be in ten years, but focuses on a much narrower vertical with one use case and one or two potential customers. That's interesting, because then I can see where the business is potentially going in the short term. It also allows the founder to show that, with the right support, they could build a big international business.'

Jonathan Lerner says a long-term vision is useful, but he doesn't want it at the expense of detailed focus on the near term:

'I don't have a strong view on whether founders have a ten-year plan or not. It's nice if they do, but I wouldn't expect it to be in much detail because people can't really predict what'll happen.

'It's always nice to see where a company is going and there is definitely time and space for that somewhere in an investor pitch, but you need to move away from the sort of hyperbole that tends to come with "Here's our vision" back to "This is what we are doing today, what we have proven and what the next three to five years look like." What's the execution plan that is going to get the investor their return? That's the window that everyone looks at and gets, because it's a bit more in front of them.

'The vision's great as that's what people get excited about. It might get their 10x or 100x return, but it's not going to get the 3–5x. What gets 3–5x is just execution.'

Russell Fisher uses a start-up's vision to help him judge whether Nationwide is the right venture partner for them from a values perspective:

'We love mission-driven, purpose-driven businesses. If your start-up's ambition is to be acquired by Amazon in twelve to eighteen months, it's probably not for us, and vice versa. But if there's a wrong you're looking to right, if there's a societal problem you're trying to address, we'll absolutely get on like a house on fire. And that's a real trend we're seeing in founders, in their missions. We see a close alignment.'

If you're a product founder, Samit Patel, Founder of Joopio Product Marketing Agency, says investors want to hear about your vision to find out what your revenue potential is:

'Investors want to know if product founders can come up with more than one product, or if they're a one-trick pony.'

The Funky Appliance Company is a case in point. It started out with a funky iron, but had a clear vision early on to expand that range and is now launching a funky kettle and funky toaster at a major tradeshow. When you're selling a long-life product, such as a kettle or iron, showing you can develop other products which will turn people into repeat customers is important.

From a founder's perspective, Heather McDonald of WooHa Brewing says you need to be specific and focused:

'You have to know where you're going. This is something that I find to be invaluable. What do you want to accomplish? So many people, if you ask their strategic goal, reply that it's to grow the brand. That's not a strategic goal. You need to put hard numbers against it; you need to have two, maybe three parameters at the most. And that's it. What is it you want to get out of your brand? Once you know that, you work backwards, and you then start to build it up.'

Credibility

Investors care massively about the credibility of founders, so one of the things that can ruin your chances is a vision that isn't credible. There are several ways in which a vision might not be credible – production timelines, assumptions on customer acquisition, profit forecasts… the list is long. The further out you detail your vision, the less likely you are to appear credible. As Jonathan Lerner explains here, it just isn't possible to plan in detail that far out:

'How are you going to be really big? You're not going to write a financial plan to get there because it will, by definition, not be credible. There are so few companies that go on to be unicorns, the rational voice would say, "That doesn't make any sense."

'And how have those unicorns got there? It's step by step, by step, by step, so you need a vision of where you can get and how you can be really big and valuable. But all your detailed plan has to do is take you from point A, where you're at now, to point B.'

The key for a credible vision is to use the fade approach I covered earlier: detail three years, summarise five years and high level ten years.

Maths

Investors use your vision as a cross-check to judge how much money you might need. They'll then look at the amount you're trying to raise and assess whether that's enough or too much. If they feel you've missed out potential costs or wildly overestimated things, it will damage your case.

Exit

There's one other piece of your vision you need to think about – how you will return investors' money to them. Georgie Hazell, head of engagement at Augmentum, a fintech-focused VC that invests at series A and later, says:

'A clear route to exit is crucial. The VC model of backing high-potential, high-risk businesses is built on making money through management fees and carried interest, and it's important to show you're thinking long-term.'

You can generally return investors' money in three ways:

- Initiating a share buy-back, using the company's own profits to buy them out
- Exiting (selling) the company in part or whole
- Launching an IPO

The IPO option is only suitable for some companies, and share buy-backs are relatively rare due to the amount of return the investor is expecting. Generally, the main option is an exit, which is another reason why planning out your vision is so critical. You need to start thinking about the exit sometimes years in advance to ensure you have an attractive proposition by the time you're ready to hang out the 'For Sale' boards.

A clear route to exit doesn't have to mean a specific timeline and exit valuation, at least for some investors. Depending on how early an investor is joining, they may be looking for different things.

Chris Adelsbach is more focused on how long founders plan to stay before trying for an exit:

'I want to make sure that I speak to somebody who is not saying, "And in two to three years, when we sell this company...". No one wants to hear that so early when they are investing;

it's almost a turn off. It could be seven to ten years before there's any type of exit, so I need to make sure that the founder is so excited by their business and the vertical they operate in, they have the potential staying power to stick with it for a long period of time.'

Jonathan Lerner says exit is about understanding the context that you're operating in:

'It's always nice if a founder has a good appreciation of where their technology would fit within the major corporates that might buy their business and why, strategically, they might buy it. As a small company founder, it's often difficult to see where the exit might come from, so we probably put exit a little bit more in defensibility (we'll cover this in Chapter 8), if that makes sense. We say, "OK, who's going to come and do what you're doing? And if you understand it really well, do you understand what the people around you are doing, especially the larger organisations? Is this something they're interested in?"

'On the one hand, if they're not interested, the corporates are not going to compete. On the other hand, they're not logical buyers if they're not interested. Is it that they can easily do what you do and have some advantages that will let them come into the market quickly? How do you defend against that? Is it just that they should buy in because they don't have the capability to do what you do or they've got a bad track record of doing that sort of thing internally?'

For Luke Lang, context is also important, but from a mergers and acquisitions (M&A) perspective:

'The reality is that investors know it's difficult for a business to speculate or pinpoint an exact exit strategy and how that might unfold, because the world just isn't that simple. If you're able to demonstrate that there have been M&As within your market to show that there is consolidation, that there is demand for M&A and your product, that can be a strong indicator for investors.'

Conversely, Vanessa Tierney's experience as a Co-Founder of Abodoo has been one of detailed requests around exit plans:

'Investors want to know that an exit's definitely going to happen, the timeline and the forecast purchase or sale price based on multiple examples of what other companies in your space have done. This can be tricky. Smart working, remote working, is new and there are not many technologies for this space. You just have to show relative technologies for investors to go, "OK, you have a clear plan." And the thing is, you might not have one exit. It might be IPO, it could be a merger, but you need to have one to answer investors' questions.'

Dan Bowyer is Co-Founder of SuperSeed, a VC that specialises in software as a service (SaaS) and AI business to business (B2B) propositions, typically investing up to £500k in seed-stage start-ups. While he understands that plans may change over time, he expects founders to have a good idea of an appropriate exit plan:

'I expect them to say, "We want to be sold to Adobe within five years for $50 million because of these reasons, and here are the goals and steps that we are going to take to get there."'

In reality, not many exits are complete acquisitions through big trade sales – they're often nuanced, with different mechanisms like earn-outs included, but that level of detail isn't expected (or possible to predict) this early on.

Approaches to exit are highly subjective, and this is where building relationships with investors in advance is incredibly useful. You can find out how they approach tricky topics like exit, and understand what will worry and what will reassure them.

In addition, the more mature your company gets, the closer you will be to your potential exit, so it becomes easier to be clear about timelines and potential valuations. A pre-seed company founder might give a rough timeline and expectation of strategic acquisition by a big player in their market, but a company in late series A or series B already has valuation, revenue and profit trajectory, and will likely already have had several acquisition approaches, so it's much simpler for the founder to articulate timelines and potential exit routes.

Before we go on to step two of the Investor Ready Roadmap, structure and scale, here are the key takeaways I hope you've gained from this chapter:

- A vision is made up of several parts

- Investors use your vision to evaluate you and your company

- You will need a clearly defined vision to complete the rest of the preparation process

Once investors understand your vision, the next thing they want to do is look under the hood of your company and check its structure and scalability. This is what we'll cover in the next two chapters.

SIX

Step Two – Structure

I t's useful to think of structure as the solid foundations of your business and scale as the house you build on top. This chapter will be dedicated to structure, while Chapter 7 will look in detail at scale.

The structure of your business is critical to its survival and ability to grow. From an investor's point of view, structure is a huge credibility indicator to how well you can actually run a business. Even with a great idea or product, without the right structure in place, you might never get investment.

Heather McDonald shared how much of a difference the strength of her business structure made for WooHa Brewing:

'What was really important was that we were thinking like a big company, even though we were small. The management was there, the corporate governance, and these things matter. When we spoke to larger investors, we had backbone in the company, and that made a difference.'

Of course, if you're at pre-seed, there will be different expectations of how much you should have done compared to someone going for series A or B. Everyone, no matter what stage you're at, has to have plans for all the things we're about to discuss. How far you are down the road of implementation will depend on your business maturity and investment stage, but if you can show well-thought-out plans, it gives investors comfort that you know where you're going and why.

In this chapter, we'll be covering:

- Basic legalities
- Business model
- The importance of Team
- Risks and dependencies
- Diversity and bias
- Corporate responsibilities

Basic legalities

This is the bedrock of your company. You need to make sure that all these things are done properly:

- You've fully incorporated your company
- You've issued shares properly
- You've set up business insurance
- Your ICO registration is complete
- Your HMRC registration is complete
- Your VAT registration is complete (if required yet)
- You submit accounts on time
- You pay taxes on time
- Your management accounts are fully up-to-date (not strictly a legality, but definitely good business management)
- Business decisions are recorded as minutes of Directors' meetings (not just investors will look for this, but also organisations like HMRC, should you ever be investigated).

Business model

Business models are many and varied, and you can look at all the types through different lenses. To give an investor's perspective, we're going to split it into two parts: your physical business model and your customer business model (we'll deal with product revenue model in Chapter 8).

It's important that your business model fits your market. If your potential customers are all over the UK and you open up a single bricks-and-mortar shop with no online selling in Cornwall, then your business model is not matched to your market. The distribution requirements of your market are key to choosing the right business model.

Physical business model

This is all about how people find you and the size of the market you can reach as a result. Investors will be interested in this because it directly affects operating costs and revenue opportunity.

Let's look at some examples:

Bricks and mortar. Your business requires customers to physically enter the premises to buy your product – a traditional butcher's or baker's shop is a good example here. Your operating costs are potentially high because of rent, business rates, utilities and the amount of staff required to cover your opening hours. Your revenue is restricted to people who are fairly local to you – foot traffic or people willing to drive a short distance for your product – unless you have a market differentiator so substantial that people will travel huge distances for your product and you can charge a premium as a result.

Tom Kerridge's pub restaurant, The Hand and Flowers in Marlow, is a great example of a bricks-and-mortar business that is oversubscribed with customers. Because of the level of experience of his staff, people travel from all over the country and the business can charge a premium as a result.

E-commerce. Your business has no physical customer premises, and your products can only be bought online. These may be tangible products, like clothing, or intangible products, like software and apps. Potentially this means much lower overheads than a bricks-and-mortar business, although you might still require stock storage space. It can also, depending on your product, provide access to a much larger market, with lower costs to reach that market. You may sell through your own site or through other platforms, like Etsy, Ebay and Amazon.

B2B software. Whereas e-commerce can be thought of as off-the-peg or customise-by-formula, B2B software is often a more bespoke business model with an element of consulting to ensure the product meets the client's need. Examples can include things like payment processing, productivity software and compliance software. You don't have to have a physical premises (although it adds credibility). Although your website will be used for information and some sales, a lot of your sales will be completed via person-to-person meetings, so your major overhead might be your sales team.

Bricks and clicks. You have a physical premises and sell your products online as well. This combines the credibility, and the overheads, of a bricks-and-mortar business with the reach of an online business – Next and Argos are among the leaders in this field.

Franchise or licencing. You may have your own physical premises or rent space at other premises, such as sports grounds. You then franchise the business out to others who either own or rent premises to run their exact copies of your business in different geographic locations. McDonalds and Starbucks are the masters here.

Customer business model

This is basically how you engage with end customers – directly, indirectly, or not at all. Understanding this will affect how you set up your company structure and how you seek to engage your market.

B2C is a direct business to (individual) customer relationship with no intermediaries. This might mean selling bacon to customers of your butcher shop or selling jeans through a website.

B2B is when your product will only be used by companies and not individuals, so you are selling from one business to another. Accounting and payroll software are good examples of this.

B2B2C. Business to business to customer is a model that exists when a product is sold to a business that then packages it up into its overall customer offering. It will usually involve white-label products that can be rebranded to the purchasing business's brand, whether it's baked beans that are sold as own-brand in supermarkets or budgeting software that is packaged into a bank's personal account offering.

You will often get hybrid models here, depending on the product, as parts of the offering may be B2C while other parts may be B2B or B2B2C. A prime example would be pension comparison software that sells as an app on a B2C basis, sells the customer data from the app on a B2B basis, and sells the app as white-label technology on a B2B2C basis into large corporates that want to provide pension comparison services for their customers.

Clarity on your customer business model helps investors understand where your major overheads are. It's also an indicator of things like length of sales cycle, which can affect cash-flow.

The importance of team

Let's start this section with some wisdom from David Horne:

> 'The number-one thing that investors are looking for is the management team – the people, their credibility and their integrity. You can have the most wonderful projections, but people buy from or invest in people that they know, like and trust. If the team is wrong, the investor won't back the business.'

There are six things to think about around team:

- Key founder qualities
- Founder vs founders
- Founder to CEO
- Building your team and managing gaps
- Building your board
- Maturing the team

Key founder qualities

Investors like certain qualities in founders:

- Being open to mentoring
- Being committed to the company

- Serial entrepreneurs (but investors are not so keen on entrepreneurs having more than one business at a time: they want 100% of your focus)

- Founders who have failed and learned

- Founders who can hire people better than they are

If you don't have all of these qualities, what can you do to fill the gap?

Chris Adelsbach says:

> 'One of the big things I'm looking for is someone who is open to mentorship. It is a really important attribute in a founder. I am looking for people who are obviously competent, but I don't want someone who is a know-it-all. I want someone who would basically say, "I am not good at certain things. Would you help me?" It's amazing when people show that vulnerability.'

Russell Fisher advises:

> 'At Nationwide, we like founders who've failed and learned lessons from it. Most of our start-up founders have at least one exit, either successful or unsuccessful, under their belt, and they can tell us the story of why they were successful or unsuccessful, and

what they would do differently. This is really important.'

Jonathan Lerner says that he looks for founders who hire people better at specific tasks than they are:

'At our stage [late Series A / early Series B], we're backing the founders more than anything else. There are a few things that we concentrate on or think are great lead indicators, and a founder's ability to hire fantastic people beneath them is a really big tick.

'If they haven't, it doesn't mean it's a red flag per se. It depends on how advanced the company is, because there's a time and a place where it is possible to hire great people beneath you. But entrepreneurs who never do that (and there are many who fall into that bucket) will struggle to scale their business, so you need the ability to understand what great looks like. Then it's not just about what you've seen; but your ability to scan the market and say, "Wow, that's what a brilliant marketing director looks like. OK, I want one who's like that."

'Hire someone who's better than you and let them get on with it. It's a really important trait.'

Founder vs founders

There is an increasing bias towards multi-founder start-ups in the early stages. For investors it means they get more expertise for their money and it spreads the risk, but founders need to understand that the dynamic will have to change as the company grows.

Jonathan Lerner explains:

> 'In the early stage, there is a strong bias towards multiple founders, which I agree with. If I was a seed-stage investor, I would want multiple founders because it spreads the risk hugely. It also means you get multiple people, ideally in multiple disciplines, who are invested in the business rather than backing, let's say, a product with a CEO where early on you'll have to recruit sales talent, which is. expensive and highly risky.

> 'But multiple founders can get messy as the business grows because often there isn't a CEO. That's fine at the early stages, but once you get to late Series A, early Series B, businesses need a CEO, so your first problem is how do the founders choose which one should be CEO?

> 'Then when they've chosen who's going to be CEO, is their friend, the co-founder and equity

holder, going to be sales director? And are they the best head of sales you could have at this stage of business? The answer is almost certainly not.

'At this point, things get complicated. The business is growing fast and taking on employees, which is difficult for the founder to manage anyway. Having co-founders involved can make it politically explosive, which is even more difficult for them and the investors to manage.

'For this reason, at Smedvig we now have an explicit conversation up front with co-founders. Who is the CEO? How does this actually work? How's it going to evolve? Even if co-CEO works today, it's not going to work in two years' time. Can founders accept that and discuss how we can take it forward?'

Founder to CEO

Maturing from being a founder into a fully-fledged CEO is quite a journey, and not one that is right for everyone. This is something Chris Adelsbach recognises:

'I realise that a lot of start-up founders are zero to one people, not one to infinity people. In other words, some people like to start companies and others like to scale companies.

'If I come across a founder who says they can get us from zero to one – great. I like that they can be humble enough to realise they may not be the person to take the business all the way to the point where they can exit. Sometimes it takes a professional manager to scale a business; it's a different skillset. Some people love to start companies and some people revel in a bit more bureaucracy, so it's about founders being honest about their own desires and capabilities.'

If the founder is going to remain in position, Jonathan Lerner feels it requires an enormous amount of self-awareness and self-development along the way:

'If you're going to be a CEO who makes it through the different raises and your business is going to grow quickly, you'll have to change just as quickly. You may have gone from setting up a business in a garage through to being a CEO, and they're two very different roles, so you need to be self-aware, constantly learning, able to delegate effectively, but still keep control, and it's a tough thing to do. Ultimately what we're looking for at Smedvig Capital is someone for whom that process never ends.'

Building your team and managing gaps

When you're creating a management team for your start-up, think of it like building a Formula 1 pit crew. Every person needs to have specific roles or responsibilities that they own while bringing key expertise to the team. The team as a whole needs to be a highly organised, well-oiled machine.

While an F1 pit crew might be split into fuel, tyres, engine and body shell, a start-up *ideally* needs seven key people:

- A CEO who can be the figurehead and build both their personal profile and that of the brand

- A chief operating officer (COO) who can look after operations and make sure the business is running smoothly under the hood

- A chief commercial officer (CCO) who can work on attracting investment and building partnerships

- A chief technology officer (CTO) who has overall responsibility for the technology, including oversight of developers etc

- A chief finance officer (CFO) who can ensure the finances and things like tax returns are all shipshape

- A chief marketing officer (CMO), which is pretty self-explanatory

The reality, though, is that most start-ups don't have this kind of management team until they get up through the levels. You do have a few options to plug the gaps, though. Some roles can double-hat, so the CEO might also be the CCO. You can build your board out to fill some of the expertise gaps, or as Vanessa Tierney found, you can make use of a highly skilled part-time resource, such as a finance director (FD) who comes into your business on a project basis or for as few as one or two days a month at a comparatively low cost:

'Instead of paying lots of money, I've started to bring in the heavyweights, like a CEO and CFO, for two, three months, and then I employ someone who's just graduate or entry level. The heavyweights set the strategy and join a monthly video meeting, but it's the person that I can actually afford who executes the plan, and it's working out really well because it takes the pressure off me as a CEO to set strategy for areas I don't know well.'

Heather McDonald has taken a similar tack:

'We've been working with a corporate finance provider for... gosh, must be four years now. Having somebody who is outside the business, who is not invested in the business, who only does numbers, is great. I have a master's in finance, but I don't have time to be FD, so it is really important to outsource.'

When you're plugging the gaps and building out your team, one thing to beware of is hiring mirror images of yourself. James White, Founder of InTouch (a CRM software company) and sales mentor, shares:

'One of the things a lot of founders do is look for people that are similar to them, rather than finding someone who is right for the role, for the purpose. They may not get on with that person, but they will do the job the founder needs them to do.'

Although you can plug gaps, Chris Adelsbach says he expects certain skills at the core, depending on the type of business:

'I generally don't invest in sole founders with just an idea; I'm looking to invest in teams. An early-stage company will always have gaps, so I'm open to that and not overly critical, but in tech investing, for example, for starters there should be someone who is technical on the team, ideally technically gifted. If I meet a team with four MBAs and a PowerPoint presentation and all the tech is outsourced, that generally does not get me too excited. On the other hand, if I meet a highly technical team that, perhaps, has a gap in sales, that's a gap I can much more readily fill.'

You don't necessarily need to have built up a big staff under your management team, although if you can show you know how to hire and lead staff, that's a big plus. Founders with prior experience of hiring great teams who just don't need a bigger team yet can make a positive impact with investors.

Building your board

Your board should be made up of your management team and some non-executive directors. Its role is to give you advice, provide constructive challenge, and ensure that the company and its directors are meeting their obligations and adhering to corporate governance. Board members' credibility should be even better than that of the management team, and they should bring with them strong networks that allow them to leverage their relationships to your advantage.

You can use your advisory board to up the experience level in your company exponentially, something Emma Ash, Co-Founder at YoungPlanet, has done successfully:

'We've got, among others, the CEO of ATG, the ex-regional vice president of PayPal, the CEO of AutoTrader, plus a partner from PWC, the chairman of MMC Venture Capital and so on. They're all people who have heavyweight experience in our sector and on our path, and we want that because they will challenge us along the way and keep us open minded about the different ways to approach things.'

You can use your board to fill management team gaps. A board member highly experienced in M&A can advise the CEO on commercial partnerships, rather than the CEO having to hire a CCO.

If you have gaps in your board, make it part of your investment requirement that you need an investor who can bring particular attributes to the boardroom. Initially, two non-executive board members is fine, but as you grow, your board will need to grow as well. Ultimately, you'll need to introduce things like audit and remuneration committees.

The important thing is that board members must be engaged with the company, not just big names on a list. Jonathan Lerner agrees:

'There are lots of people who have advisory boards with some big names, but it doesn't actually achieve anything as a value to that company. If they're not engaged in the company, they really don't know the business properly.'

Russell Fisher feels the same:

'Having a decent advisory board or group of non-executive directors doesn't hurt at all. But if they're there for their names, if they're not actively engaged, there's no point. It doesn't impress us. We ask what they bring to the table, why haven't we met any of them? If they're so engaged and we're a potential investor, why are we not speaking to them?'

Joe Sillett, Co-Founder of The Funky Appliance Company, took a specific approach to building out his board, bringing on existing highly engaged investors first, and then seeking out expertise that rounded out the board profile:

'For our first funding round, Sadie and I, a husband-and-wife team, took our concept and idea out to an investment base that had signed up on an equity crowdfunding platform. Having got the investment we needed and gained the initial army of people supporting us, after round two, we were then thinking, OK, how does this business present itself in an even more confident and professional light? And what is required for us to do that?

'After our second funding round, we felt that the two lead investors, who had put in a significant portion of the investment up to that point, at least deserved a place at the top table. Going into the third funding round, we felt that the board could benefit from some extra expertise in the consumer electronics space. One of the investors in the second round was Peter Groom, who was behind the successful Flip Video venture that ended up selling to Cisco. He also brought Fitbit to Europe, and he's now the European Sales Director for Tile. Peter came on board between round two and round three.

'After round three, the management team thought it would be nice to have some specific appliance experience, so we met Guy Weaver, who had been in the appliance industry for thirty years. He came in after round three. And now in the deck for the series A funding, people can see what this team is made of. Is the management team behind The Funky Appliance Company capable of delivering what it's saying it wants to deliver? My answer would be a resounding yes.'

Be brave when it comes to finding board members. People are often flattered to be asked, and the worst they can say is no, so work out who your ideal board members are and target them directly.

Maturing the team

Much as the CEO's role changes, who and how you hire will have to change too over time. You'll go from hiring all-rounders who'll get stuck in to hiring specialists, a transition that Heather McDonald made with WooHa Brewing:

'In 2019, I started hiring people specifically for jobs. Our new production manager has a degree in brewing and distilling from Heriot Watt and four years of professional development training from Marston's. He was hired to do all the analytical production manager work.

'Our new sales director, Scott, has got international experience with Red Bull, BrewDog, Carlsberg. We're looking to bring on board people who aren't learning on the job. We're looking to bring on board people who have been there, done that, bringing experience and their network with them.'

Investors looking at a start-up moving out of early stage and into scale-up mode will want to see maturing of the team built into your fundraise, specifically which roles you'll be focusing on and whether you've accurately benchmarked the proposed salaries.

Risks and dependencies

Part of a strong company structure is a clear understanding of risks and dependencies. Here we'll look at some key examples, but you'll need to carry out a full assessment of your own company.

For investors, one of the biggest risks is that start-ups are based around a few people. It only takes one of them to leave or become ill and the whole thing can tumble down. To an extent, it's a risk investors have to accept, because start-ups can't afford all the people and processes that more mature organisations have, but there are some simple things you can do to reassure investors you're at least thinking about the issue.

If your key people are technology related, then insist on full code-security banks, IT architecture and maintenance documentation. This reduces the risk by enabling someone else to step in if needed. Customer relationship management (CRM) systems put in place right from the start ensure that whole networks of potential customers won't go out the door if someone leaves with the information in their head. Making sure that key passwords are known to all of the management team is also critical. Quadriga, a Canadian cryptocurrency firm, made the news in December 2018 when founder Gerald Cotton died unexpectedly, without leaving anyone able to access $190 million of his customers' money in cryptocurrency and fiat funds.

Likewise, a single supplier that you're completely dependent on, with only a single site, creates a huge risk for your business. What if they get flooded, suffer a fire or go bust?

A good way to review the people area of risks and dependencies is to look at each person on your team and ask, 'If they walked out the door tonight and never came back, what would happen?' That should tell you where your risk areas lie, and then you can figure out what to do to address them as well as you can. You can take a similar approach for suppliers and key business data.

Diversity and bias

Another important consideration for your management team, your board and your overall recruitment is diversity. Even though start-ups are, well, starting up, there's disappointing evidence that the same lack of diversity present in much older companies is manifesting itself – Atomico's State of European Tech Report 2019 showed the proportion of women in executive positions in venture capital-backed companies has fallen to only eight percent and over 84 percent of founders self-identified as white.[10] Let's be absolutely clear: diversity in the workplace is not about box-ticking or quota-filling. It's about bringing diversity of experience to bear for the good of the company.

---

10 www.atomico.com/presenting-the-2019-state-of-european-tech-report

If your management team is made up of people who all fit the exact same profile, you risk bringing bias into your management decisions. By excluding parts of your target demographic, you risk not having the knowledge or experience within your team to understand how a decision you make might affect parts of your client base, and are putting your company at a disadvantage.

Georgie Hazell says:

> 'At Augmentum, we look for teams who deeply understand the needs of their customers, and it tends to be the case that the more closely the team demographic resembles the target customer base, the better. Diversity of thought across the management, wider team and board is crucial to good business, and this is increasingly being scrutinised by the best investors.'

I personally find it hard to understand why diversity remains such a blind spot for many companies. If you ask senior leaders in a large corporate what they would do when expanding into a new market, their answer is likely to be, 'Get local expertise, someone who has knowledge, experience and credibility in the area, and put them at the front. It will ensure we don't make mistakes, and makes it clear to the new market we are taking into account local requirements, rather than wading in from afar.' Diversity in boards, management teams and staff is just the same – make sure you have the right knowledge, experience and credibility across your target client demographic.

Diversity is particularly important when you're expanding into a new market or seeking to expand an existing market. Gaming is an area where diversity is starting to make a dent – the stereotypical single male who was the target of most computer games for quite a long time excludes a huge part of the potential market. By making their teams diverse in gender and culture, some gaming companies have been able to build games that attract a far wider audience than the stereotype and expand their existing market.

Bias

An emerging concept that may well need to be in place in your company is a bias control. The last thing an investor wants is a viral scandal because your product demonstrates clear bias for/against certain groups of people. If you're using AI, machine learning and natural language programming, or even a standardised manual process, you need to show that you've thought about bias and have clear processes and tests to ensure unfair bias does not exist.

Show your planning and testing against four specific areas:

- **Framing the problem:** ensuring there isn't inherent bias in how the problem is framed in the first place

- **Data collection:** the data with which you train the algorithm must come from sufficiently diverse sources to prevent bias for or against particular decisions or groups of people

- **Data preparation:** when you're telling the algorithm which data to consider and which to discard, there is another opportunity to introduce bias

- **Training and testing:** once you start training and testing the algorithm, you need to be constantly watching for instances of bias which may show up in the results, and then digging in to understand why they happened and correct as necessary

Remember, not all bias is bad. If you run an organisation seeking to provide development loans to companies based in the UK, for instance, and the algorithm declines companies based outside the UK, then that is an intentional bias you can set. Monitoring, training and testing for bias should be an ongoing obligation as the algorithm continues to learn. This ties back to the earlier point about diversity – by making sure your management team and your staff base are diverse, you will automatically help to avoid bias by having input from a more diverse range of people.

Corporate responsibilities

Corporate responsibilities can be complex, especially if you're operating in a regulated area like pharma or financial services. Your policies, processes and controls contribute to the control framework of your company (how you are identifying and managing risk), and this is something corporate VCs in particular may want reassurance on, as failure to manage your corporate responsibilities could blow back on their own brand.

There are layers of regulatory and legal compliance you need to observe: formal layers such as licences and approvals, and informal, but just as critical, layers that protect you and your customers on a daily basis. You also need to ensure that you aren't just compliant in your country of incorporation, but in every market you interact with. You don't even have to be trading in a market to be caught by compliance rules.

Health and safety

Even if you're using a co-working space, you're still responsible for the health and safety of your employees. This can cover everything from wellbeing policies to making sure desk space is correctly aligned to prevent back pain and neck strain. Staff training and understanding your obligations as an employer are critical.

Data privacy

Data privacy has become a huge topic over the last few years. The introduction of the General Data Protection Regulation in the EU in May 2018 sparked a global wave of data privacy legislation, with major fines being issued to British Airways (£183 million), Google (€50 million) and Marriott International (£99 million). The last thing you (or an investor) want(s) is to see your name added to the list of breaches and fines.

In the UK, make sure you're a registered member of the ICO (www.ico.org.uk) and get expert guidance on how to ensure you are compliant. Even your ICO registration is something you need to remain vigilant about – as your staff numbers increase, you're required to change your registration details, answer different questions, take on different responsibilities in some cases, and pay more for your registration.

Cyber security

There are currently no formal licences or approvals for cyber security, so instead it falls under the daily vigilance category. You need to be able to prove to investors that you have carefully considered cyber security and taken all steps possible for your circumstances to protect your company and your customers. That may cover things as basic as making sure all computers and laptops are protected with anti-virus software and encryption, to ensuring you use hosting providers with the best in cyber-security protection. You will also need regular staff training on how to spot things like phishing attempts.

Policies

When you run a fast-growing start-up that relies on agility and speed of response to keep going, writing and adhering to a whole bunch of policies may feel a bit stifling, but it's something investors will probably request as part of your due diligence pack. You don't need a policy for every single thing that happens in your business – usually a blended risk- and regulation-based approach works well.

Start by looking at your company and all its key processes. Where are the risks of something going wrong? Once you've identified your risk areas, look at which regulations require specific action by your company. From this, you can create a set of policies which help your current management team and staff all work to the same standard. This will massively assist you when you grow your team further and onboard new people.

Several companies now offer 'get started' policy packs. SeedLegals, for instance, provides a pack that includes an employee handbook, employee privacy policy and website privacy policy.

Staff training and certification

If you operate in certain sectors, your staff may be required to hold qualifications and certifications for them to be allowed to do their jobs. While you might sidestep the issue initially by making sure you hire people who are already qualified/certified, longer term they are likely to need to keep these requirements current, so you must be able to show that you are supporting staff to maintain their qualifications and keeping records of required certifications etc as part of your risk-management approach.

Some of your policies may be so critical to your business that it is wise to have proof that staff have completed the training and attained a certain level of understanding, perhaps through completing a test. In financial services, this particularly applies to areas such as know your customer, anti-money laundering and sanctions.

As your business matures, it's worth going for certifications such as ISO. They require that processes and staff within your business set and maintain certain standards. In some industries, bigger players in particular won't work with you unless you have the relevant ISO certification.

Crisis management

Investors will want to know that the business has the capacity to continue even in the face of unexpected events, so you'll require evidence of backup routines, failovers, code-security banks, plans for cyber-security attacks, and fire or flood planning for yourself, or if your suppliers are similarly affected. You should have a plan for every dependency in your business, whether it be your staff, the internet or your supply chain. You will need a plan not just for managing during the crisis itself, but also how you'll exit that crisis and cope with any long-term impacts.

By this point, I hope you have a good understanding of how to structure your business. Now let's move on to the second part of step two of the Investor Ready Roadmap – scale.

SEVEN

Step Two - Scale

Investors and customers will both want to know about your business's scalability – investors because there is no way they will achieve a 10x return if you can't efficiently scale your business, and customers because they need reassurance that you can handle their business. Ultimately, though, scalability is about creating a company that is in great health and able to meet the demands placed on it.

Dan Bowyer says scalability is often the least well-formed area of start-ups he works with:

> 'It's a bloody mess. There are probably some issues, which we either support or consult or coach founders with. You really have to work out how to systemise selling, building, doing,

delivering, software. It's hard, but people generally confuse growth with scale. We need to change that – they are not the same thing.'

Dan's point is a good one and highlights why scalability is often, in his words, a mess in the start-ups he helps. Growth and scale are *not* the same thing. Growth is turnover, customer acquisition and the front end of your business, whereas scale is the back end – how your company runs, its systems and infrastructure. Without scaling the back end of your business effectively, you could find costs spiralling out of control, growth stopping, or the company facing serious reputational problems as you're unable to handle how fast your business is growing.

When you scale well, revenue increases while costs remain low, driving greater profitability. The user experience continues to be of a high standard, staff morale is strong and the underlying technology is robust and stands up well to the pressures of fast growth. In addition, efficient scaling de-risks the company when it's in high-growth mode, by tightly managing costs and performance. This will help to regulate cash-flow – something that can really trip people up. Scaling needs to cover every stage of your business cycle as well as pure back-office functions, such as payroll.

Whether you're at pre-seed, seed or series A, you need to have plans for scalability, just at different levels of maturity. At pre-seed, you haven't built anything yet, but you must be able to show how what you're going to build will be structured for scalability. At seed, you should have an MVP and be starting to generate traction, so you will be testing and refining your scalability model and putting in place the next steps that will allow you to expand. At series A, you're in the thick of high growth and should already have some scaling in place, with more improvements to come.

Now is a good time to take what I call the scalability test. If your business tripled or quadrupled overnight, could you handle it? How long would it take you to have everything in place to handle that amount of business smoothly? If you haven't done any scale planning before now, the answers are probably a resounding no, you couldn't handle it, and it would take months to get things running smoothly (some companies never achieve a scale model that works and continue to run with high costs and lower than necessary profits).

With the importance of effectively and efficiently scaling your business front of mind, in this chapter we will cover:

- Business model scaling challenges

- Scaling quickly to cope with big clients

- Scaling options

- Manage and monitor

- Product, people, process, assets and technology (PPPAT)

- The only way to prove it is to do it

Business model scaling challenges

You may feel more pressure in different areas of your business depending on the type of product or customer base you have. If you have a B2C product – something like a budgeting app – then you will be dealing with thousands of different individuals, one person at a time, so you may feel more pressure in the lead generation space in terms of volume. If you have a B2B model where you create white-label pension advice for large corporates to deploy to thousands of their staff globally, then you'll be looking at overnight massive growth from one source. In this case, lead generation isn't such an issue, but delivering on your sale certainly is.

In the B2C scenario, where you're reliant on engaging thousands, if not millions of people to generate high growth, you have a significant risk that your customer acquisition cost will make the growth unmanageable. The more you can use technology to help you cope with high growth, the better. Make your marketing highly targeted and automated, and if you can create a strong enough experience, a fully automated end-to-end sales funnel where the customer only needs to speak to a person in exceptional circumstances is ideal. Amazon is a great example of a business that has this nailed.

Scaling quickly to cope with big clients

A huge individual client could be anything from a global car manufacturer to an international bank or the National Health Service. Their common characteristics are that they employ enormous amounts of people and generate, and absorb, huge amounts of data.

There are two issues you face in this scenario:

- Persuading a customer or potential investor that you're capable of scaling up
- Scaling up quickly enough once you've won the work and/or investment

A multi-national bank, for instance, needs reassurance that a two-person start-up based at WeWork is capable of meeting its needs. When a massive customer is thinking of scale, they're thinking of four things. Can your business cope with the amount of data? Can you meet their operational demands on your company (support, contracting, etc)? Will your product stand up to the required level of usage? Will you still be in business next month?

Mark Abbott, CCO at Supermoney, a company that provides next-generation accounting ledger technology, says convincing corporate clients and investors of the company's ability to scale has been one of his toughest challenges:

> 'The biggest problem is global companies putting their trust and money and agreement into a company made up of two guys, and that's it. Although we have a development team that we are bringing in, the global companies' concern is, "We can see what this technology can do but you are still a start-up of two individuals".'

Scaling options

Too often, high-growth companies throw people at the problem, which means their costs rise in pace with or even outstrip their revenue. Looking at full-time equivalent (FTE) – a unit that indicates the workload of an employed person – vs revenue or FTE vs profit is a good way to understand how well businesses have scaled over time. Ultimately, if you can systemise your processes well, you shouldn't need to throw people at the problem. Although you will certainly need to hire some heads as your grow, efficient processes should keep that to a minimum.

You'll gain further benefit if you can automate as much as possible, too. Your other option as you scale is to outsource, making the headcount issue someone else's problem – this works particularly well if you can outsource entire processes or functions of the business, with only a 'head of' in the business for oversight and management.

Heather McDonald says WooHa Brewing Company only kept in house things that were core to the business:

> 'Small companies can do an awful lot with out-sourcing. Brand development, artwork – we outsource that. What we kept in house was the stuff that we knew we needed to do that was important for the fabric of the business, such as all the export. We send out our laboratory testing, but we manage all our export docu-mentation, because we need to have that spe-cialisation within the company.'

Joe Sillett and his wife Sadie have created an almost entirely outsourced model at The Funky Appliance Company, with just the two of them at the centre:

> 'We manage everything in the office here, but we have a big team of people around what we're doing. We have an outsourced logis-tics and warehousing fulfilment company – a good business based in West Sussex that we've worked with for a long time now – to do all of our fulfilment, so we don't get involved in any of the warehousing when the orders come

through in real time. They go through to the system, the orders get picked and packed that afternoon, and they go out the door in the evening. It all happens seamlessly; it's part of a virtual jigsaw puzzle.

'We've worked with a PR agency over the last year to get our name out there and generate publicity and profile. A digital agency works on our behalf, delivering traffic from Google to our website. We also have a specialist Amazon agency managing our Amazon store. These tasks could have been in-house; we could have spent thousands finding a warehouse somewhere, and then we could have gone out and hired people, but when you're growing a small business, I've always favoured the approach of doing it on a lean model basis. Engage outside experts and turn the tap on and off and pay accordingly; don't bring too many staff in too early when you can't justify the expense.'

Manage and monitor

The important thing when you're scaling is to figure out how to retain oversight. Make sure the alarm bells ring if the process isn't being followed or is failing in some way. Rather than micro-managing and checking everything that everyone does, this is where business key performance indicators (KPIs) come in. If something is important to you, it should have a KPI pulled to a central dashboard that gives you a full, hopefully real-time overview of the company.

For Joe Sillett, a key KPI might be 'length of time between order placed and package dispatched to customer'. He doesn't need to stand in the warehouse and monitor people; he just needs the packing company to send the data to him.

Product, people, process, assets and technology (PPPAT)

We've talked about why scaling is important and some of the options you have; now it's time to dig into what you might need to scale, and the challenges you'll experience along the way. These are all challenges investors are well aware of and may ask you questions about. We're going to break it down into five areas: product, people, process, assets and technology.

Product

Scaling your product is about meeting market demand. How you scale will depend massively on the nature of the product. A physical product such as an energy drink is all about production and supply logistics, so your concerns will be about suppliers' capability to scale when you need them to and the cost implications of that. A tech product may have different considerations.

Georgie Hazell says:

'We (as investors) want to know about the scalability of the tech as well as the business model more broadly.'

There are six factors that, at a high level, are important for tech scaling:

- Ability to cope with user numbers (overall and simultaneous users).

- Data storage and data recall requirements.

- Overall system accessibility requirements (white labelling to multiple large corporates could need different interfaces with different requirements).

- Market expansion complexities – if different markets (people or geographies) require different rules, you are building complexity into the codebase.

- Code manageability – is your technology coded in a way that will stand up to continuous development by multiple developers?

- Architecture expandability – cloud hosting makes it easier to bolt on capacity, but you still need to architect technology in a way that makes that possible with minimum manual intervention and cost.

You should have a clear product roadmap that shows how your product will evolve over time, both by building in additional functionality but also by building in scalability to cope with additional markets or growth within existing markets.

People

This section splits into three areas: customers, employees and other stakeholders.

Customers. Nailing the customer experience every time while scaling fast is incredibly hard to do. As soon as you can afford it, I would highly recommend you get a head of customer experience on your team – preferably someone with plenty of background in high-volume adoption and creating experiences that delight. They will pay for themselves ten times over in the first six months, both by ensuring new customers stay because they loved their experience and by causing those customers to tell their friends and bring new custom in at zero cost to the organisation.

Customer support is a really important subset of customer experience that must be scaled well. Revolut, one of the neo-banks that is in high growth, was under fire in 2019 for its customer support. With more than double the amount of complaints to the Financial

Ombudsman than any of its challenger bank rivals, Revolut took the step of setting up a customer support phone line, where previously it had relied solely on online chat tools. This will have been an unplanned cost in the company's scaling, but it could have been foreseen if the teams had engaged with their customers earlier.[11]

Just because you want to scale your company one way doesn't mean your customers will enjoy that experience.

Employees. There are five challenges that can happen with employees when you're scaling:

- Your existing employees get overworked and stressed, and either leave, make bad mistakes, or both.

- You're so busy changing everything about the business as you grow that you're thrusting constant change upon your employees, so they don't know whether they're coming or going. This can result in stress and resentment.

- You realise that your employees are not as driven as you and aren't working at the pace, or in the way, you imagined, so your plans for growth and scale are being hampered.

---

11 www.thisismoney.co.uk/money/markets/article-7075509/Revolut-complained-small-online-bank-Financial-Ombudsman-Service-reveals.html

- You struggle to find new talent to hire at the standard you need, which slows you down.

- You need to onboard new hires quickly and in large numbers, but you aren't equipped to do it well. Then your operation slows down and you risk work being done incorrectly.

How can you create, and demonstrate to investors, a scalable employee model? You need to be able to tackle all of the listed issues through forward planning. Here are a few suggestions:

- If you've got existing employees, get them involved in the scale planning. People who feel ownership are always more engaged.

- Work hard at offering flexibility and perks and building a great culture. If you never mention how you will manage your growing employee group to an investor, they're unlikely to invest in you – without your people, you're nothing. What Julian Hearn has done at Huel is a great example of clear employee culture – staff at Huel are called 'Hueligans', and from day one, thanks to good communication, they know exactly what it means to be a Hueligan.

- Start building digital assets like e-learning and operations manuals sooner rather than later. They make it much easier to onboard new employees and ensure consistency.

- Use your existing employees to carry out quality assurance on your new ones until they are up to speed.

- Engage with a range of recruitment agencies, and do it far earlier than you think you need to. If, according to your plan, you'll need new people to start in December, then kick off your recruitment searches in May or June to make sure you land the right people in time.

The final part of the employee puzzle when it comes to scaling is being clear about how the role of the management team, and in particular the CEO, changes. When your business is a two-person outfit, you'll each do everything, but as you grow, it's important that the CEO steps into a full CEO role, and allows the people they've employed to take over the coding, or the marketing, or the sales.

It's vital the CEO spends their time at the strategic level, effectively laying the track fast enough for the company train to keep accelerating. Likewise, each member of the management team must be able to move into oversight of their area, rather than delivery. The start-ups that manage this well, usually by checking themselves regularly, are the ones that will fly, whereas start-ups with senior people still fiddling about in the detail are never going to gain the same kind of traction. Their leaders will be looking in the wrong direction – down, not up.

Other stakeholders. This is a wide and somewhat loose grouping as I'm using it to talk about organisations and their expectations as well as individuals.

Regulators in each of your markets will have a vested interest in your scalability. New rules might apply if you grow beyond a certain size, and as you expand into different markets, then new regulators come into play. Part of your scale planning has to include how you'll engage regulators up front and regularly to ensure you are ahead of the curve on compliance and aren't caught out, as the effects can be devastating. Massive fines and removal of licences to trade are just a couple of the possible outcomes if you do not keep pace with compliance demands as you scale. If your product supply chain will involve multiple jurisdictions, you also need experienced tax advisors on the case to make sure tax costs are being properly managed and not duplicated.

Suppliers must be able to keep pace with the demand your company will generate, so just as your investors need proof of scalability from you, you must gain the same from your suppliers. If you are tech-based, your main suppliers might be your hosting provider and website/social media team, if you have one, whereas if you manufacture an actual product, then all your component suppliers, plus logistics and your manufacturing capacity, come into question.

Investors and shareholders will need formal updates on progress as you scale. Showing you understand the need to brief and involve this community is never a bad thing.

Process

Your business processes are at the core of your ability to scale. If you attempt to scale a bad process, you will soon find out how small issues become big ones.

At Spark! my team uses a visual equation to help companies work out the end result they are trying to create when scaling process:

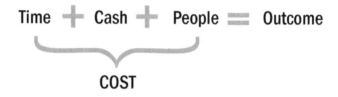

We start at a single outcome – one customer successfully onboarded, for instance – and figure out the cost of achieving that outcome in terms of time, cash and people. Then we figure out how to increase the number of outcomes on the right-hand side while keeping the cost side of the equation as low as possible. The aim is that the higher the number of outcomes goes, the cheaper it gets to deliver per outcome – the age-old principle of economies of scale. While it's easy to get a discount on a box of bananas as opposed to buying a single piece of fruit, figuring out how you create economies of scale within a process can feel more challenging.

There are two steps to scaling a process. Firstly, create the leanest possible process with the least amount of steps, and secondly, work out the right way to deliver it. This might mean automation, outsourcing or just hiring people to do it instead of you.

Creating the lean process first is critical. Good processes are simple, not over-engineered. The only steps included are the ones necessary to achieve the outcome. Steps always need to be focused on the outcome, and never how a particular person would like the process to run. There should never be more than one layer of review for anything – either you trust the people you've devolved responsibility to, or you need to get some new people.

There is an important lesson to learn here from some of the global corporate players, as Steve Jobs demonstrated at Apple. Stripping things back to the bare minimum, requiring 'simple as standard', he allowed a huge company to be agile and generate speed to get Apple ahead of the market. Many large corporates, particularly in regulated industries, are so tied up in red tape that they find it incredibly hard to move anywhere. Even if your market or industry is heavily regulated, working with regulators to understand how you can be compliant while running the simplest process possible is a great approach.

You may not show an investor all the individual steps of your process, but if your current process is 100% manual and you demonstrate that you want to use some of the investment money to reduce the process down to four steps and automate three of them, you will give the investor confidence that a) you understand what scaling means and b) you know how to achieve it. Likewise, by showing that areas like marketing are data driven and highly targeted, not scattergun in nature, you can demonstrate that your marketing processes are cost effective and aren't going to drive costs through the roof.

Assets

If yours is an asset-driven business, then scaling it will involve figuring out how to acquire assets as quickly and cost effectively as possible. If you need more cars for your limousine service company, for instance, can you use a fleet lease arrangement rather than go for full capital outlay on each car? For every type of asset, you need to design a repeatable acquisition method that will deliver economies of scale, cost and time to acquire.

Technology

Aside from your actual product or service, how you use technology to drive efficiency in your business operations is important in your scaling plans. So many technologies now have the capacity to link with each other through application programming interface (API) connections, so there is massive opportunity to connect up systems and remove the need for manual intervention and the risk of human error.

It's worth getting some specialist advice on this, as it can save you so much money and time in the long run. This kind of expense is usually 'good spend' from an investor perspective, because you're increasing company efficiency and reducing risk. Using technology well can be as simple as showing that you employ an online project management tool, like Monday.com, which can be expanded to accommodate additional team members and clients as you grow.

Automating parts of your sales funnel is a great way to show scalability as well. Initial marketing that drives re-targeting of the leads to a self-service trial setup or an automated booking process demonstrates efficiency.

The only way to prove it is to do it

The only way to prove for certain that you can scale is to do it. If you *haven't* scaled yet, all you can do is show you understand exactly where the pressures will be, you have a credible, executable plan, and you have expert help to ensure growth is unimpeded, costs and risks remain low, and you'll fully meet the customer's needs.

A plan is great, but just like your product, you'll need to build, test and refine your scalable business as well. Show how you will measure success, when you will review and include alternative options in your plan; it all helps.

There are no shortcuts to achieving scale; it requires detailed attention to every aspect of your business on an ongoing basis, although as you build out your team, you should be able to devolve much of the attention to detail to others. Use your business metrics to help you make decisions based on data: how long does it take to currently move a potential customer through the sales funnel and why? What causes customers to leave/stay? Why does the payroll process take fourteen days instead of five? All of these help you adjust and adapt your scale plan.

While planning how you can scale may feel complex, actually delivering on it is even tougher. As a founder, you must have support through the high-growth phases. Apart from your board, get a mentor, a business coach, or join a mastermind group. It can all help. Spark! offers a founder support service that provides strategic and operational support for businesses in high growth, precisely because my team and I recognise how hard it is.

This brings us to the end of step two of the Investor Ready Roadmap, and we've covered a lot. Both structure and scalability should have helped you see four things:

- What you need

- Where you are now

- What the gaps are between now and what you need

- The importance of having a plan to close those gaps

Now we're going to move from the back end of your business to the front end: your market and product.

EIGHT

Step Three – Market

In this chapter, we'll focus on:

- Being clear on your brand
- Product/market fit
- Defending your market position
- Go-to-market strategy

Being clear on your brand

There are a million books out there on creating a brand, so I'm not about to get into the detail of that. Instead, I want to cover why brand is important and what it means for investors.

Your brand isn't just the colours you use and your logo – it's much bigger than that. Brand is about being easily identifiable, building familiarity and creating customer experience – all of which ultimately boil down to trust. Your brand can tell customers whether you are right for them or not. Historic brands like Coutts (a private bank founded in 1692) won't appeal to the same people signing up for Starling Bank, one of the fresh new challengers.

Being inconsistent in how you apply your brand can lead to customer confusion and dilution of market impact. Investors like to see a strong brand consistently applied that is capable of building a following and creating customer trust. When it's done well, brand clarity equates to higher revenues and higher valuations.

Product/market fit

Validated problem + validated solution + people who will pay, in a vertical you can access, that isn't already saturated

What is product/market fit (PMF) and how do you know when you've got it? PMF is when you put the right product into the right market in a way that causes 'pull' from the customers. You don't need to hard sell because they are queueing up to get to you. iPhones and Harry Potter books are great examples of where this has happened, and currently start-ups such as Huel and What3Words are showing meteoric growth because of their PMF.

This is a key area of focus for investors. If they don't believe your PMF is realistic, you won't be getting any money. You may not achieve the perfect PMF straight away, but if you've done your homework, you'll be able to pivot as you validate and get closer and closer to the right fit. If you're early stage, you probably won't have traction to demonstrate PMF, in which case you'll need to rely much more heavily on research and small validation groups.

There are eleven different areas to think about when it comes to PMF:

- Market size

- Market growth

- Product durability

- Competition

- Market responsiveness

- Accessibility

- Need

- Pricing

- Niching

- Return rate

- Product revenue model

Let's look at each of them in detail.

Market size

Your overall possible market, or 'total addressable market', is basically all the people who experience the problem that you solve and may want to buy your product or service. Investors generally want to see two things: credible statistics that prove the overall size of the market and (ideally) information from your company showing how much of that market you've already captured over what time period.

This is how Emma Ash put things together for YoungPlanet's investment deck:

> 'In our investment summary deck, we used a lot of current facts and figures to explain the size of the problem and how our app can help address that problem. We also had nearly a year's worth of data of our app's performance within one single London borough, which demonstrated the significant growth potential. This made a compelling case for investment.'

Nic Brisbourne shares Forward Partners' approach to market potential:

> 'Most companies that we turn down are rejected because their market size isn't big enough. We assess market size in three stages.

First, we examine what we think is the truly addressable market for the product and whether the product will be able to scale. Secondly, we look at whether the product could take a sensible percentage of that market – our rule of thumb is 10%. Finally, we calculate whether that is going to be enough revenue for us to get an exit deal worth around £60 million. We do this analysis for all companies, however big or small.'

If you get turned down by an investor because your market size isn't big enough, it doesn't mean your business doesn't work; it means the investor thinks it won't be able to grow big enough to return 10x investment. You then have a choice – amend your market to find one that *can* generate a 10x return, or go for a different financing route. A business that makes a 5x return can still be massively profitable, fun to run and give you a great lifestyle, so there's no shame in this.

Market growth

Investors prefer products in growth markets because a) they're areas where people are prepared to spend money, b) the possibility of investors getting a good return is increased and c) the market is likely to be durable for some time – again, vital if you are to sell the company at a good price in a few years.

Market growth can be triggered by social change (more people want electric vehicles to help the environment), legislation (all people who work outside an office become required to wear high-viz all day) or population growth (your shop in a little town used to have an addressable market of 2,000 families, but a new housing estate has just been built with another 500 homes on it). Alternatively, new markets can be *made* by some products. No one knew they needed, or wanted, a touch-screen mobile phone until Apple made one, and then a massive growth market was born.

Product durability

We've all seen the latest app crazes on Facebook – ageing you up, turning your head into an animal etc. Their product durability is less than a day – once you've aged yourself up once, you're done and you won't use it again (unless the first picture was so bad you're trying for a better one).

If an investor thinks your product could be a one-day wonder, there is no way they will invest money. They want long-term growth.

Luke Lang agrees:

'It's important to be able to demonstrate that the market opportunity exists and is not going to be a flash in the pan. There's a good example in Cowboy. The company has had to demonstrate that the demand for and rise of e-bikes is going to continue, it's a trend that is going to persist, and Cowboy will be able to take a decent chunk of that market.'

Competition

Competitors in your market are companies that offer the same, or similar, outcomes, but not necessarily the same product. A good example is a market where the outcome people seek is to get fit and healthy. The competitors in that market could be sports clubs, gyms, yoga studios or swimming pools.

Investors want to know who your competitors are and why you're different and better than them, as Nic Brisbourne explains:

'For product, you want something that is going to be clearly different, and this is where we push. We're product-driven investors, and for us that means having a clear idea of who is going to buy a product and why it can be connected to the next 10x exit.'

It's a good idea to research each key competitor, and then use the data to help you build a positioning map that shows where you sit against them.

When you're talking about competitors, it's important to show not just how many there are, but also how saturated that makes the market. Is it an existing market with well-established competitors where you will have to fight for every % of market share, or is it a virgin market where you're first to recognise a need and, for a while at least, will have an open field?

Facebook is the best example here. There was only MySpace in the market ahead of it, so Facebook exploited this heavily, to the point that now a third of the world's population has a Facebook account.

Market responsiveness

For investors, understanding how responsive your market is helps them gauge how quickly you'll be able to generate revenue and take market share. In B2C, you may be able to generate massive growth quickly because something becomes fashionable (think Fitbits) and people pile in. If your main customers are large corporates, they generally move slowly and each relationship requires a lot of nurturing before you can get a sale over the line. Sometimes it may take a year or two before a corporate will buy your product. Time to buy from first customer contact to sale is an important metric for investors, along with cost of acquisition.

Accessibility

Ideally, customer acquisition needs to be as cheap and simple as possible. For that to be the case, your market needs to be accessible.

If your main market is the elderly – perhaps you sell mobility products – it's actually a pretty inaccessible market, because elderly people use the internet far less than the younger generations and they don't commute to work where they might see advertising regularly. Most companies targeting the elderly rely on 'snail mail' advertising, which lengthens the customer acquisition cycle, is expensive and doesn't allow social media interaction in the way that the internet does.

Likewise, your market may be less accessible if your target audience is hard to identify. For instance, if you're targeting 'carers of dementia sufferers', you won't find an easy way to identify those people. It isn't a category they tick on their social media profiles, and may not even feature on their Google search history.

Need

If you can generate a high level of need, a 'must have', then you will obviously create a tighter PMF than if your product is seen as optional. Samit Patel says founders need to be aware of where their product sits in the overall hierarchy:

> 'Founders need to think about where their product would rank – will people queue round the block for it or is it a nice to have?'

Of course, someone else may generate need for you. New legislation can often force need in the B2B market.

Pricing

Pricing is a key element of PMF – have you found the magic price at which you'll retain a great margin and your customers will flock to buy your product? It can take some experimenting to get that right, as Vanessa Tierney explains:

> 'You convince yourself "This will sell", but you don't *know* until people say, "I'll buy that, and then I'll buy that for x amount." It took us ages to get the pricing right at Abodoo.'

Niching

It's always tempting to aim at the whole of the addressable market and tell investors that you will be achieving market domination across it all, but in the early days at least, targeting and achieving PMF with one niche creates a great base to scale up from. It means you can focus your marketing and refine your sales funnel to attract only that niche. Once you have that nailed, then you expand.

As an example, at Spark! we could say that our whole potential market is all start-ups, globally. And eventually it may be, but what we started with is a niche market of London-based tech start-ups between pre-seed and series A – a big enough market to allow us to test and refine our products before we expanded.

Emma Ash says YoungPlanet is niched by market geography:

'We started in Hackney to see how much traction we got, and within our first year we reached 7% of all Hackney households with families. That's exciting! We plan to grow in concentric circles from there so that we keep things moving within the community and local neighbourhoods. Eventually we hope to cover all of London and beyond.'

Rick Rowan says NuroKor BioElectronics is niched by problem:

'Our core market that we pitched in depth to is around pain and musculoskeletal disability, which goes into occupational health, back pain being the number-one disability globally. It's also the number-one reason for days off work.

We've had huge amounts of success in treating that.

'Of course, that's a bit like saying GlaxoSmithKline are good at doing pain relief. Yes, they are; they also do a load of other things, as do we, but the scope of the market is so big, it becomes incredible. That's why we niched it down into the pain and musculoskeletal market.'

James White found the problem with failing to niche is how much it costs to achieve customer acquisition in a wide market:

'We did a piece of work to actually look at what industries we covered by percentage – the highest we got was 4%. I used to tell people this was great, because if anything were to happen to any one industry, it wouldn't matter. But it was also our biggest weakness, because we were a small business, and we were everything to everyone and not something to someone.

'I tell people now that I blew a quarter of a million quid in marketing by being too general. And you can blow money quickly via Facebook and Google and every other marketing company that will take your money all day long.'

Return rate

If you have a small market and the thing you make will last a lifetime, your customers aren't going to return. In fact, your sales will dry up fairly quickly – not attractive to investors. Even in a large market, if people tend to only buy or use your product once, it can be a problem, depending on how much the market increases in size over time.

Gillette has solved this problem neatly. Although the main razor handle it sells will actually last several years, the razor blades won't, so customers have to keep coming back to buy more blades.

Joe Sillett tackled the problem at The Funky Appliance Company by bringing out additional products in the range so people return to buy the matching kettle or toaster. KitchenAid, a company that makes iconic kitchen mixers, has brought out a wide range of accessories that don't come with the main product, so people then come back to purchase a dough hook or a balloon whisk attachment. Whatever your tactic, the important thing is to figure out how to make your company or product 'sticky' so that customers return again and again.

Product revenue model

The product revenue model describes how you actually make money from your product. Your revenue model needs to fit your market and your product type, to help create that all-important PMF. There are all kinds of revenue models you can use; here are just a few examples:

Data monetisation business model. Companies like Google, Facebook and Money Dashboard monetise data rather than charging their customers for their service.

Social conscience business model. Buy one, donate one – this business model appeals to a specific customer niche, where people are willing to pay more for the product they want, to gift another version of it to someone in need.

Core + accessories/consumables model. Sell the main product – for example a razor – and then generate repeat custom through razor blades.

Go-between/aggregator business model. Airbnb, Lastminute.com and Moneysupermarket.com are great examples of this business model. The business actually has no product of its own; it provides a service that links customers and businesses, and its power is all in its matching algorithms.

Freemium business model. The basic version is free, the premium version charges for additional features/data or for removing advertising. This model usually applies to apps where you can upgrade to premium within the app by paying a fee – think Fitbit, MyFitnessPal and the Tube Map app.

Affiliate marketing business model. Affiliate marketing is a revenue model that purely makes money from advertising – the content itself is free, but the adverts played to the users generate the revenue. High traffic websites like Mumsnet, TV channels like ITV and major YouTube channels like 'Yoga with Adrienne' make their money this way.

Subscription business model. The subscription model usually works in one of two ways: either the company provides all the content/effort and users continue to subscribe to see the content/use the service (Netflix, Amazon Prime), or it's some kind of software that users put lots of information into, and then have to keep paying to use their own information (Monday project management, QuickBooks).

Consulting business model. Consulting is one company paying another company for advice, so users are actually paying for a combination of people and knowledge. Accenture, McKinsey and, of course, Spark! are good examples of this.

Within all of these models, you can decide to provide the discount or the premium version, and your market and specific niche may add a particular flavour to your version. In addition, your business model could be a combination of some of those listed above – a subscription model that does some affiliate marketing and sells data on its consumers to other companies is a good way of maximising revenue streams. It's also perfectly normal to start with one business model and add others in as revenue streams later.

Now that we've considered all your options around PMF, the important thing is to think about how you'll validate against them. Validation is critical. It proves your idea has legs, and it proves to investors that people will be willing to pay for your product or service on an ongoing basis.

You need to get to this point as quickly as possible, so you can amend your approach if your customer feedback is that your current plans won't work. It's a basic tenet of lean start-up methodology – test with the smallest amount of built product or information, and then keep doing it as you iterate to ensure you stay on track.

Samit Patel warns to make sure that you are actually validating with your ideal customers:

'Don't just validate with your friends and family. It's really easy to come up with a basic prototype and get out on the street and just ask people.'

He feels lack of validation – 'Not validating the idea, testing the product. Not understanding the size and durability of the market or how much people will want the product' – is a key reason why start-ups fail.

An aspect of validation that Jonathan Lerner looks for in late series A/early series B companies is making sure the product is actually solving the same problem for lots of people:

> 'In B2B, it's about making sure that you have at least five clients, ideally ten, so it's not one massive contract, and that what you are doing for each of them is the same. From a software perspective, this means you haven't created bespoke things for each client; the clients are all using your product for the same thing. Sometimes you could have a single piece of software code, but each client is using it to solve slightly different problems, or a variation on the same problem.

> 'For me, that always rings alarm bells. Do you have proper PMF here? Because actually, the sales process for each client has meant they've bought the same thing for a slightly different reason. That probably indicates you can't just hire a sales force and scale the product because there is no singular "Here's the problem we're solving. Here's why we solve it really well, etc", there's a multitude of them. That makes the problems your product is solving very different, which means scaling will be difficult.

'A single problem that gets solved multiple times for multiple different clients is the ideal. And then the extension to that is "Are there a lot of potential clients with that problem within the geographical remit that we're already covering?"'

Now is a really good time to stop and reflect. You started out with a vision of what you wanted to achieve, but now that you've fully considered your PMF, you may need to go back and readjust. Are your growth and scale dreams possible in your market? Have your potential customers indicated they would be happy to pay your proposed prices, or do you need to revise your projections?

It's often at this point where founders have to stop and reconsider, and possibly pivot their offering to account for what they've found in their research. If you do change direction because of what you've found, don't feel downhearted. Every business pivots as it grows, and changes based on quality validation are actually a great thing to share with potential investors – 'We started here, we did our research, we found x, y, z to be true, and as a result we changed a and b. We're now starting to get traction.' It shows them you don't just forge ahead regardless, but instead take a considered and data-driven approach to managing your business.

Defending your market position

Defensibility is a huge deal for investors. If you can't defend your market position, and your product within that, your company is worthless, as Samit Patel points out:

> 'How easy is it to copy? How defendable is your market? Fidget spinners were copied so quickly and easily, the founder had no market left to defend.'

There are three approaches to defending your market position:

- Barriers to market entry

- Registering your intellectual property

- Creating competitive advantage

Let's look at these in more detail.

Barriers to market entry

These are usually barriers created not by you, but by either legislation or the demands of the market. For instance, if you work in a highly specialised area, you may need certain certifications as a company to be able to complete that work, and your staff may need qualifications or experience. The more limited the pool of qualified people is, the harder it is for another company to break into the market. Likewise, if components of your product are rare or hard to create, this can also act as a barrier.

Registering your intellectual property

One of the most effective ways to protect your product and your brand is to use formal intellectual property (IP) registrations. Once your patent, trademark or wordmark is registered in a jurisdiction, no one else can use it and you can defend it legally against people who stray too close to it.

From an investment point of view, if you show that you have already protected your IP, or are in the process of doing so, it is a positive count in your favour. Equally, investors will want to know that you aren't infringing on anyone else's IP, so get all the searches done when you register your own IP to help confirm that.

Not having your IP fully protected can come at quite a cost, with legal bills to challenge cease and desist letters running into tens of thousands. It's worth using a specialist IP protection company to help you register everything properly – IP can be a complex area of law, but it's so important to your company, it's not an area I recommend you tackle on your own, particularly if you need overseas IP registrations as well.

If your business is such that you can't protect your IP in these formal ways, you need to be able to explain to investors in a credible way how you will stay ahead of the crowd.

Creating competitive advantage

You can achieve competitive advantage in a few ways:

- Being first into a market and gaining significant market share before anyone else enters

- Creating something so complex that other companies will struggle to copy you

- Being so innovative as a company that you are continually inventing new and improved products that keep you ahead of your competitors

Rick Rowan gave his view on the race to stay in front:

'A lot of investors are concerned about proprietary IP, but some of the biggest companies in the world, even the unicorns, don't necessarily have proprietary IP. They're just doing things in a particular way that the market loves, saying, "It doesn't matter whether anyone copies us, they're only going to copy where we're at now. We're pioneering, we're up at the front, we're doing things that nobody else has done, and will continue to do so."'

Rick's right. The only caution here is that a big player in your market, with far more resources than you, could decide to start doing what you do, and may be able, just by having more money, to overtake you. You need to show investors that you're aware of who could do that and whether they're showing any signs of moving in that direction.

Go-to-market strategy

You've identified your target market, you know who your customers are, and you know how you're going to defend your market position. Now you need to show an investor how you're actually going to engage with your market in a go-to-market strategy.

What is a go-to-market strategy?

It's basically a plan that shows how you will take your product to market. There are lots of elements that combine into your strategy, some of which we've already covered (like brand). At Spark! we look at go-to-market from a customer journey perspective, covering every step from product awareness to closing sales, and we use this model to help us stay clear on what needs to happen when.

Close...   **Sales**   **B**

Drive...   **Interaction**   **R**
                                      A
                                      N
Generate...   **Awareness**   **D**

Ultimately, you need to shape all of this into a sales funnel. If a potential customer engages with your social media, does it link them easily to where they interact with your product ecosystem? Depending on your product, you may have a fairly short sales funnel, or you may have a more complex one for a more expensive product.

For example, you may hear about Elon Musk in the news, follow him on Twitter, decide from one of his tweets that the Tesla cars look pretty cool, go to the website, do some more reading about specs, maybe check online reviews as well. Then you may book a test drive, look through a brochure, and finally you may buy a car.

The important thing is to validate with your customer base what steps they feel they would need to go through before they would commit to buying, and then ensure you create this flow in as seamless a way as possible. Showing investors that you understand your customers' buying needs and have addressed them, or have a solid plan to do so, really adds credibility.

How much of your go-to-market strategy you've actually put into action will depend on the stage your company is at. Nic Brisbourne explains his expectations for the early stage companies he looks at:

'It's stage dependent. Some of the investments we make are just an entrepreneur and a plan. The entrepreneur is often working evenings and weekends, and it's not until they sign the term sheet and hand in their notice that they go full-time. We wouldn't expect much from those early-stage companies over and above a well-researched concept. With later-stage companies, we're looking for momentum with customer acquisition and revenue.'

By laying out the plan, you help yourself and an investor understand how much your go-to-market strategy will cost. This is something that concerns Russell Fisher:

'The go-to-market piece is a constant worry bead for me with a lot of start-ups because they bring out a chart, saying, "We're at this level", and I see the inevitable hockey-stick graph and say, "That's great. How are you going to do that? How are you going to step up behind that?"

'I seem to be speaking to a lot of companies that are developing propositions direct to consumer, and I keep saying, "Do you understand how hard it is to get the number of customers you want to get when you're going B2C and you're doing it through Facebook ads and social media? Have you any idea of the burn rate on that?"'

Samit Patel agrees:

'I often see people not allocating any or enough funds for marketing. Driving people to the product is hard. It's like building a shop, designing it, making it look all pretty, but how you drive people to the shop is key – it's almost harder to market it than to build the product.'

Generating awareness

It's vital that investors see how you are engaging with your market, and how you're actively positioning yourself within that market. This is the front end of your sales funnel, where your customers get to know you and your product.

Before you start putting together your plan, it's a good idea to assess where you're at now. Searching for your company, words associated with your product, the problem you solve and the names of your founders on Google is a useful way to do this. Ideally, you should be all over the first page, but the likelihood is, you won't be. In this day and age, you are who Google says you are, and if you aren't at the top of search results, you may as well not exist.

Deborah Lygonis feels her visibility and the visibility of her company, Friendbase, is vitally important:

'At the end of the day, clients want to see what's going on out there. We write on social media – we have an active community on Facebook for our members, we use LinkedIn a lot. I tweet and make sure that I tag certain organisations that I know will retweet. So yeah, we are really trying to be out there.'

Rick Rowan hasn't started with much on social media yet, but NuroKor's product reviews are building traction for the company instead:

'We are gaining huge amounts of traction by way of social proof. We've got five-star reviews on every channel that grow daily with amazing stories.'

Depending on your market, you can sometimes get out there on foot, as Emma Ash explains:

'In 2016, we organised a big swap day in Hackney for people with children to come and exchange some of their outgrown items for new ones. The feedback was really positive and we were impressed by the quality of items on offer. At this event, we were able to capture people's contact details, so we had a user-base to launch with once the app became live.

'As the app gathered momentum, we made contact with some of the "superusers" (people who'd listed several items on the app) and organised focus groups with them to gather feedback, both good and bad. This brilliant group of individuals then went out and spread the word at all their various baby groups and with their Mummy friends. So far we've had 95,000 app launches, and over 6,500 unique users.'

Social media of some kind is a must and investors will definitely check to see how you are engaging with your market through that medium. If you're a B2B business, size of following isn't quite so important, but if you're a B2C business, then evidence of community size is vital.

Content marketing, where you publish content to attract potential customers, is increasingly important, although again it's dependent on your product and market. If you're at a point where you have an MVP and are gaining customer traction, then investors may want to know what advertising you are doing on social media. You need to be able to articulate this clearly – geo-targeting, profile building and re-targeting based on views are all key.

Traditional advertising (TV, radio, newspapers, professional publications) is expensive and often not tightly targeted towards your market. Investors would not typically expect to see you advertising in these types of media while you are still in early stage, but if you can generate awareness via free means, like being interviewed on the radio and having articles published, then it's all to the good.

One of the key ways your start-up can engage with its market is through its founder. The old saying 'People buy from people' is still true: on Facebook, Richard Branson has 3.2 million followers, but Virgin only has 343,000; on Twitter, Elon Musk has 31 million followers, but Tesla only has 4.8 million. Founders should be posting regularly on social media, sharing sneak previews of products, speaking at events and generally creating a positive impact for themselves and their company.

Being visible in your market doesn't just attract customers, as Vanessa Tierney found:

'Probably the biggest change in the last five, ten years is that most investors, especially at angel and seed level, are on social media themselves. It's not like a VC that expects a team to go and research how prominent you are.

'I had one investor, and by the time I actually spoke to him, he said, "Yeah, I've been following you for months. You've had loads of publicity, you've been on national television." It nearly threw me because I didn't realise how far reaching some of the publicity I'm doing is.'

Creating visibility to investors can be particularly important in the run-up to a crowdfunding campaign. Many companies will engage a PR agency at this point, an approach that Joe Sillett followed:

'If I think back to pre-launch last year, we were clear that we wanted to bring a PR agency on board. A lot of the early work that we did with the PR agency involved gifting, competitions and getting the word out in the right kind of media. We worked with several magazines and ran competitions with them to win one of our products; we didn't have the money to spend tens of thousands of pounds on placing full-page ads in glossy magazines or running television adverts, but we did manage to get our product visibility and column inches through competitions. This is a really good way to drive awareness and interest in your product.

'We did quite a lot of that type of activity at the beginning with the PR agency and on our own social media sites – Twitter, Facebook, Instagram – trying to target people who had an interest in ironing. We were approached by JCDecaux, the leading outdoor media company, inviting us to be part of the "Nurture Scheme". JCDecaux would match our contribution free of charge to deliver double the advertising space. That was a good result and in the end we had digital billboards at Clapham Junction, Victoria, Liverpool Street Station, Euston, Birmingham New Street, Manchester Piccadilly and Glasgow Central. That campaign ran for two weeks, which generated a lot of awareness. For a young brand and business, this was a great way to build our profile at railway stations.

'We also targeted several leading newspapers and online bloggers, with the hope of having them review our funky iron. If you look at the "In The Press" page on our website, you will see that we were successful in getting some great coverage in *The Telegraph*, *The Independent*, T3.com, iNEWS and other leading sites.'

Emma Ash and YoungPlanet hired a PR agency as well:

> 'During the Crowdcube campaign, we employed an agency to help us generate some press to raise our profile, because we needed a specific portfolio of contacts to do this. We were fortunate and had a couple of high-profile pieces, including one in the *Daily Mail*, "This Is Money", and one in the *Sun*. Some of the press enquiries were initiated after a profile in the *Hackney Gazette*, so local press is just as important.'

Something else that is great for raising awareness, among both customers and investors, is awards. There are hundreds, if not thousands of awards you can enter for, and having an award or two under your belt is great credibility and shows investors that other people in your market are taking you seriously.

The main issues with awards are finding ones which fit your business and the time it takes to apply for each one. There are companies that will do all this for you, but as always, they cost money.

Driving interaction

Once a potential customer is aware of your product, you need to interact with them in some way before they will buy. This might be a meeting or a call, but there are other things you can provide too:

Brochures. If you run a tech company, brochures may seem a bit old hat, but if you have any kind of personal interaction with your customers, they are worth their weight in gold. They add credibility and a sense of professionalism, and they give people something to take away with them which fully describes your product in your own words.

Brochures are particularly valuable if you have a B2B model and have pitched to one person in a business. They now need to go and explain your product to others before they can get purchasing signoff.

Community building. Investors will want to see evidence of the community you are building around your product. Do you have a Facebook or LinkedIn group that you update regularly, full of people who are engaged with your product? Have you been able to build a solid mailing list of people who want to hear about what you're doing?

There are lots of low-cost ways you can engage your market that show investors you have reach and inbuilt feedback mechanisms, which are vital. You can ask for beta-testers on social media and run a proactive beta-test phase where you capture feedback. Assuming it's positive, you can then use that in quotes all over your website and social media. You can set up customer feedback groups, online polls, contests, online product tours, and even run some events to which you invite as many of your ideal customers as possible and demonstrate to them.

Closing sales

You'll need to be able to show investors how you carry out sales as well. At an early stage, it may be just the founder doing the selling, but as you get up to series A and beyond, as Jonathan Lerner explains, more is expected:

> 'As a company gets to mid B stage and certainly C stage, we would expect a fully functioning sales engine where you can just put fuel in. What we're asking at the earlier stages – I guess the "red-flag process" – is "Has there only ever been founder sales?"
>
> This is only in the B2B world. In B2C, it works differently, because you (the founder) are doing what you have to do to sell straight away and it's not founder sales by definition. And then you're looking for depth of channel. Have you found one particular channel which is brilliant for you, but clearly isn't going to scale, or are you just getting a small niche within a massive channel?

'People who want to work in B2B, it's all about "Have you scaled away from founder selling?" Our observation is that founders can sell the dream, and they can sell it really well. But then their business struggles because salespeople *can't* sell the dream, they can only sell a product. And the better the product, the easier it is for them to sell.

'If you've got a salesperson, even if they're not a brilliant salesperson, and they are selling the product, that says a lot about the business and the product that you've created and the need for it and the PMF. Founders blur the lines of PMF because they're selling the dream. They're basically selling stuff that they haven't built and won't have built for the next twelve months. And that is quite common with enterprise software.

'When there's a long development, long implementation time, OK. But what you can't do is sell different things, be pitching different things to twenty different customers, because then the product is never going to go in a linear direction.'

Market visibility and maturity has to be taken into account. Jonathan Lerner explains how he evaluates this:

'Everything has a positive and a negative. There's a positive of having no market visibility. Say you're doing really well – you now have £2 million revenue and are still growing quickly. You have PMF across, let's say, ten companies that are doing the same thing. Your sales are growing well. You've got a salesperson, so it's not just founder sales, yet you're not out there and your website sucks.

'Actually, I would feel quite positive about that. You're doing well already, and we can see a clear gap where we can help.

'On the flip side, if someone is good at product marketing, we're buying into a known capability that we then don't have to recreate. The red flag on either side would be a company with lots of slick product marketing, but it's not growing as quickly as it should be. That's a problem. If a company has no product marketing and is not growing quickly, that's still a positive because it can do more. But why hasn't it done that already? It shows lack of self-awareness on the part of the management team or founder. There's a gap they haven't appreciated, they don't know what great looks like, and that is a problem.'

Overall, investors are looking for a solid go-to-market strategy and evidence that it's working. Much like a product roadmap, your go-to-market strategy will mature over time, as you get more money and resources. It can be helpful to show how this will happen to investors.

This chapter has been all about clarity and evidence:

- Being clear enough on your brand that it becomes an asset in its own right

- Being specific about your markets and having evidence to prove you can impact on them

- Having clearly defined IP that you can prove is well protected

- Having a clearly defined go-to-market strategy that you can demonstrate is correctly targeted and making a positive difference

Now that we've looked at the front-end growth of your business, it's time to look at the numbers.

NINE

Step Four – Numbers

In this chapter, we're going to be covering several kinds of numbers that are relevant to both you as a founder and potential investors. These include:

- Financial statements and management accounts

- Unit economics and other KPIs

- Forward projections

- Valuation

- Cap table

- The raise

Financial statements and management accounts

Investors will expect to see all your previously filed statutory accounts. Even if you haven't been required to provide a detailed profit and loss to Companies House, they'll want to see that too. You'll also need to provide up-to-date management accounts for the current year – it's a good idea to include explanatory notes for any non-standard income or expenses that might raise an eyebrow.

Unit economics and other KPIs

Unit economics are basically a summary of everything it costs to deliver a product or service and what you can sell it for per item, which will reveal your potential profit margin. If your business model relies on large numbers of sales, investors would often expect to see improvements in profit margin the more products you sell, because you can make savings through economies of scale. If you're early stage, unit economics may be projected because your business is pre-revenue, but as you progress, the numbers should be proved by your management accounts.

This is something Jonathan Lerner says is critical:

'At Smedvig, we would definitely want proven unit economics, so what you're doing needs to make economic sense. It can't be a case of, "Oh well, it will get better over time." We don't subscribe to that; we want to have proven unit economics and a review that says, "We think these figures will stay as they are, maybe they'll get better here, they might get worse here." In other words, we want a view of how they will evolve.'

If you can't demonstrate a commercial approach to your business, you won't win investors, as Russell Fisher explains:

'A lot of start-up founders seem to fixate on the problem they're solving or the thing they've built and think it's absolutely brilliant. It's wonderful to see that passion, but they've got to think about the commercial angle of it as well. Otherwise their solution will never become a reality, and that's sad.'

Having KPIs (metrics) that you actively use in running your business is both a great credibility builder and a fantastic way to ensure you know exactly what is going on, all the time. Ideally, all metrics pull into a single dashboard that allows you to drill down into the detail where needed.

Metrics matter to investors, as Russell Fisher explains:

'We [at Nationwide] do financial modelling on investment. We apply a methodology to look at what return we think a business can come back with and what that's driven by. We want to understand the metrics that matter to the business, often asking founders, "How many customers have you got? What's the average spend, the sustainability?" These are typically the three key numbers. Then we ask, "What are the metrics that matter? What do we believe has to happen to those metrics to make them successful? Does that look realistic? What has to be true?" and stress test that.'

There are two types of metrics to consider: day-to-day metrics and success metrics. A success metric is basically a target, eg 'We will hit one million active users by the end of 2020'. It's something an investor will want regular reporting against, so be careful what you list as success metrics and what timelines you give to them.

Now let's cover some of the key day-to-day metrics you may choose to focus on.

Burn rate. This is how much money you spend per day/week/month. One of the most critical things for start-up founders is how quickly you'll run out money, so understanding your burn rate and what that means for your cash reserves is important.

Cost of customer acquisition. This is the cost to get a customer through the door for the first time and signed up to a sale. It could include marketing costs, time spent talking to them, and cost to you of any free products they use on their way to becoming a customer.

Overall revenue. This will show your month-on-month sales figures, whether they are increasing and how they match up against projections. If you have more than one salesperson, you will want revenue split by salesperson so you can understand if one is generating more sales than another, and why.

Recurring revenue. This is a subset of overall revenue. If you have a business that can generate recurring revenue, then it's important you show how much of it you're getting – the higher the proportion of recurring revenue, the more you can assume customers like your product or service and will remain loyal. This is a great indicator for investors.

Revenue and profit per FTE. This is actually two metrics, but they're great for tracking whether your company is successfully scaling. Good systems, processes and technology should mean revenue and profit per FTE go up as you scale. They certainly shouldn't go down – if they do, something is wrong.

Customer retention. This one is particularly important if your product is pre-revenue, for instance a freemium app where you've only launched the free part so far. Even though you can't demonstrate revenue figures, you *can* still demonstrate how much customers like your product.

NPS. This is basically a customer satisfaction score. There are many ways of calculating it and lots of different sources from which you can pull it in, from customer feedback surveys to social media commentary and thumbs up/thumbs down indicators built into your software. When you're starting out, customer feedback surveys, plus a few focus groups with customers in exchange for a voucher or similar, are probably enough. You can expand on the detail in this area as your business grows.

Invoices payable and due to be paid. You need to know what needs to be paid and by when, who should be paying you, and if they're late. This is your 'exposure' metric, because it's totally focused on money that either you're about to send out of the company or that hasn't come in yet.

Cash in the bank. A basic one, but also critical. You want enough in the bank to cover all your liabilities and provide a buffer for emergencies (ideally at least three months running costs), but not so much that your money isn't working hard enough for you and could be better deployed elsewhere. Setting a range, and tracking where your money is within the range, can help you understand where things might be going wrong in your business processes.

Your overall sales funnel metrics. This is a collective of a number of metrics that tell you how well your sales funnel is working and whether you are spending money in the right place. It measures things like clicks and downloads on your website, engagement with your content (either on your website or via social media), engagement with any free gifts or trials you offer and conversion to customer rates.

Customer lifetime value. This is a calculation of how much a customer is likely to spend with you over the time that they use your company. For instance, if your business is a food subscription box, you know that the customer pays £20 a week and the average customer stays with you for at least eighteen months – so your customer lifetime value is £1,560 (£20 × 78 weeks).

Investors will potentially use these metrics in combination to understand the strength if your company's position. For instance, low cost of acquisition and high customer lifetime value is a positive indicator.

Forward projections

Your forward projections are a big deal to investors. They expect detail and they hope for credibility, based on sensible assumptions and evidence.

Too often, investors are presented with a hockey-stick graph that shows an amazing skyward surge as soon as the start-up gets the investors' money. The only place those get filed is the bin. Investors expect at a summary level that you'll present revenue, costs, and earnings before interest, taxes, depreciation and amortisation (EBITDA), with detailed breakdowns available behind them.

Heather McDonald says being comfortable with the numbers is vital:

'I would definitely recommend that people understand the financial side if they go speak to investors, especially high net-worth investors, because chances are if investors have grown and exited a company, they are *very* comfortable with the numbers. And the numbers need to work and make sense.

'At WooHa Brewing, our model runs through to June of 2023. We've always run about three to four years of financials, depending on where we fall in the financial year, and we've done that in line with staff growth as well.

'It's about taking a lot of time to look at how you want to see your growth curve. What's the importance of gross profit? What's the importance of net profit? What's the importance of the turnover levels, top line versus bottom line? Who do you need on the team to execute the projections?

'It becomes easier and easier the longer you're trading. I can tell you right now, the plan for 2023 is that we'll have forty people on staff. Twenty will be sales staff, and of those, fourteen will be international, six will be domestic, and we'll have four tap rooms in specified areas.'

Joe Sillett has a similar approach, with a real focus on detail and transparency for investors:

'Each time The Funky Appliance Company has presented to investors, we've had a five-year roadmap with a full set of financials. I sit down with a top accountant and spend two days going through a spreadsheet to make sure it is fit for purpose and that anyone analysing the spreadsheet can understand all the thinking behind what is going on and the costs of the business and the sales assumptions. What are the goods going to cost? What are we going to sell them for? What is the margin? Who are we going to sell them to, and where? Will that be on Amazon or eBay, in stores or our own website?

'Quite a detailed level of planning goes into each round. Our pitch books and financial spreadsheets have always been on point and at the level that they needed to be, because we can't go into any investment round without having done that work properly.'

Valuation

Valuing a company, especially a start-up, is a weird mix of a highly scientific approach and the subjective opinion of the valuer. Russell Fisher says his experience at Nationwide is it comes down to the underlying risks and assumptions:

'What we're doing is testing assumptions and de-risking as much as we can, so we have an assumption on what we want the answers to be. Do we understand the business model? Do we understand what needs to be true or believe it will be true? The numbers will be the product of all of that.'

There are lots of different methods to value a company, but some of them are only appropriate for mature or asset-heavy businesses. The four methods I see used most often in the start-up/scale-up ecosystem are benchmarking, the VC method, discounted cash-flow and multiples.

Benchmarking

This one does what it says on the tin – you find other companies similar to yours, in either the same or comparable sectors, and use them to approximate a value. Benchmarking is often the most sensible route if you're pre-revenue because you don't have much else to base a valuation on, unless you have inherent value in any proprietary technology you've developed.

Deborah Lygonis used the benchmarking approach when putting together a valuation for Friendbase recently:

> 'We benchmarked a lot with other companies in similar situations, coming up with a fair valuation in comparison to our competitors. That's what investors have accepted when we've talked to them.'

The VC method

Also useful for pre-revenue start-ups, this method predicts the eventual sale price of the company at exit, and then works back from there to come to its current value.

Discounted cash-flow

This method is a bit more technical. Here you take a five-year projection of your company's future revenue and expenses, and use that to develop an estimate of the cash-flows. You add the five annual cash-flows together, and then discount them by a certain factor to calculate the present value of the future income stream. The discount factor can be influenced by a number of things, which we'll look at soon.

Multiples

In certain industries or sectors, there are accepted revenue multiples which are used for valuation purposes. It may be 4x, 6x, 8x – whatever is common in that industry. As long as you can demonstrate you are using the correct multiple for your industry, this calculation is fairly simple, as James White found:

> 'I based the valuation for InTouch upon other SaaS companies. SaaS-based companies traditionally had an 8x recurring revenue model, so 8x our recurring revenue equals the value. Using that as the basis, I gave three or four examples of other companies that have been sold at that rate.'

There are at least six other factors that can affect valuation:

• The founder's prior experience and successes

• The size of the market opportunity

• IP (such as proprietary technology) already developed

• Annual recurring revenue (ARR)

- Other investors pursuing the start-up

- If the sector is hot – electronic transportation as a sector is way hotter than orthopaedic shoes (my apologies if your start-up sells comfy insoles)

Many accountants will carry out valuations (at a cost), or you can try newer online solutions like Equidam to help you work out your company's worth. Once you've got that figure, decide what to do with the information. Jonathan Lerner thinks that in some cases, it may be better not to include it in your deck:

'I don't particularly like valuations in decks. At Smedvig, we will always ask founders, "Are you giving valuation guidance? What was the last round on that?" And people give different responses.

'At the moment, founders seem to be saying, "No, we're not giving valuation guidance. We'll see what offers we get." That's a sensible thing for an entrepreneur to say. And then they'll say something like, "The last round was done at x and we've grown this amount since that point", because these are real stakes in the ground.

'Ultimately the market will decide how much your business is worth, not you, especially in a young, fast-growing business. But giving comparables is helpful so you're dealing in facts rather than conjecture. If you go too low when putting a value on yourself, you've automatically anchored people to a price that may be below where they would have gone in. You've then just lost value. And if you go too high, you automatically get put in the bucket of "entrepreneur who is pushing their value a bit too much". I'd be careful about that.'

There has been some criticism of the valuations businesses can achieve on crowdfunding platforms as well, with a feeling that they're higher than would be achieved in the traditional market. As Luke Lang explains, it's not the crowd or the start-up that sets the value, but the lead investors who've already put their money in before the raise goes live on the public platform:

'A lot of the businesses that come to us already have lead investment, whether that's from an angel investor, a new or returning investor, or VC firms. In that case, the negotiations around valuation have all been done at the back end. The valuation has already been agreed; there has been a level of due diligence on that valuation. There's been a period of negotiation and probably compromise, which can be helpful in a crowdfunding environment. When people potentially query or question your valuation, you're able to point to investors that have put in a significant amount of money. Then questions or queries around valuation can melt away.'

The overriding thing to keep in mind when coming up with valuations, or even negotiating them with potential investors, is that founders want maximum cash in return for minimum equity, and investors want minimum cash in return for maximum equity. Agreeing a compromise is a complex negotiation.

Cap table

Your capitalisation table is basically a summary of who owns what shares and any special classes or arrangements attached to those shares. Investors (current and future) will want to see what the position is now, plus a view of the plan – ie after this raise, once additional shares are sold to new investors, what do all the percentage holdings look like?

The effect of dilution on the current investors' holdings etc is something Elle Berrett finds can be missing:

'Sometimes founders forget to prepare a cap table of existing structures. It's really important for investors to see a table saying, "This is the current structure, this is what I'm proposing, and this is where I want to be." Make it really clear for the investor to understand what they can expect to get in return.'

If you've got a simple cap table with not many investors so far, you could manage it in an Excel document. Alternatively, if you've got quite a few investors, you might want to use a tool to manage it and keep a full record of all the changes. Reportally and similar tools are available at prices that don't break the bank.

One thing new investors don't like is a scrappy cap table with lots of investors who all potentially want a say. If your cap table is looking a bit muddled, it may be worth figuring out if you can consolidate. A long list of existing shareholders who all need to sign off on a deal can delay it going through – you can always guarantee there'll be someone on holiday.

The raise

Deciding on how much to raise is a bit like *Goldilocks and the Three Bears*: you want not too much, not too little, but just right. Too much and you'll struggle to spend it within the SEIS/EIS deadlines; too little and you'll be running back to your investors asking for more.

To some extent, investors expect start-up founders to need more than they thought they would due to a combination of no one being able to predict the future and inexperience. Going back for more money because your growth has gone mad is one thing; going back because you didn't cost things properly in the first place isn't such a good look.

The amount you're raising should match several things: your financial projections, your valuation, the amount of equity you're happy to give up and your vision. An investor needs to be able to look at the raise amount, look at the projections, check them both against the vision and conclude that the money will be enough to reach the milestone you're aiming for with this raise.

You also need to remember to include money to cover the costs for your next raise, and a small contingency. Look for two to three months' run rate to give you coverage in case calamity strikes and you can't do the next raise at the time you planned for some reason.

Nic Brisbourne says it's important to raise the right amount for *your* company. Asking for the amount you've been told is easier to raise will affect your credibility:

> 'One of the scenarios we see is that start-up founders have been advised by someone that it's much easier to raise £1–2 million than it is to raise £500–800k, so they decide to raise £2 million, thinking that money in the bank never hurts. The problem is that their plan around what they will actually do with that money quickly becomes vague.'

Another reason why start-up founders try to raise too much too soon is that they're aiming for 'perfect' straight away, rather than an MVP. I've seen more than a few £1 million raise plans for a pre-seed start-up with nothing more than an idea to its name. That won't fly for investors.

Ed Stephens suggests something else to consider is when you'll need to raise next:

> 'Timing is sensitive. Businesses may be seasonal or sales cycles may be longer than expected, so a company founder should be acutely aware of where the cash vulnerabilities lie. Will you run out of cash in the middle of August? If so, this is a terrible time to fund raise. As a rule of thumb, school holidays are bad times to court investor attention as they are people with families and often will be enjoying time off with the kids. This will lengthen any discussion you were planning on having.'

What you're going to spend the raise on

Investors want to know that the money you get from them will achieve something specific, and they expect to see a breakdown of how the raise will be spent. One of the most common mistakes we see at Spark! is founders getting the balance wrong between product development spend and generating sales. We often see 70% on development and 30% for everything else, but a start-up's job is to generate revenue and ultimately profit, so founders need to make sure they're adequately funding sales, community building, marketing and scaling the company. Without those elements, they'll just have an expensive product that no one is using.

As a founder, you can use your raise to fund the first six months' salary for key hires – providing you've got them lined up with contracts ready and are able to push the button as soon as you get the money. Any product development you expect the raise to cover should be for something that will generate extra revenue, otherwise investors will question why you're doing it.

We've talked about lots of different types of numbers in this chapter, but there is a key principle that applies to all of them:

Every number you use must be up-to-date, verified and tied back to evidence that proves why it is what it is.

With the numbers sorted, the next step to think about is investors.

TEN

Step Five – Investors

In this chapter, we'll focus on the people who have the money you want. We'll be covering:

- The other customer
- The SEIS and EIS
- Types of start-up investors
- Creating a raise strategy

The other customer

As I mentioned way back in the Introduction, it's important to think of investors as the other customers of your business. Unlike your normal customers, they want to buy part of your company rather than your product.

Like any customer, investors respond well to clear information and good marketing. It's helpful to think of investors as customers because it demystifies them – so many early-stage founders I meet are a bit intimidated by investors. Remember that they're investing because they want to make money – they need you as much as you need them.

The SEIS and EIS

These schemes were set up by the UK government to stimulate investment in new companies and are viewed as being among the most favourable business investment schemes in the world. SEIS is for the earliest stage companies, and EIS is generally for the next stage of investment. There is also a special provision for knowledge-intensive companies under the EIS rules.

Investors will want evidence that a company has received Advance Assurance of their qualification for SEIS or EIS relief before they invest. HMRC can take up to eight weeks to process advance assurance applications for either scheme, and since 2018, applications have had to include the name and address of at least one *potential* investor. This stops start-up founders applying when they have no chance of getting funding and wasting HMRC time.

If you're doing a crowdfunding round, a signed agreement from the crowdfunding platform is enough. A three-year business plan 'of the same level of detail that you would send to your investors' is also required with the application.

How you qualify

In general, start-ups won't be eligible for either SEIS or EIS if the following criteria apply:

* An excluded activity forms 20% or more of their trade. Excluded activities include:
    - Land purchasing
    - Banking
    - Insurance
    - Money lending
    - Leasing
    - Receiving royalties
    - Legal or accountancy services
    - Property development
    - Farming
    - Woodland ownership/management

- Shipbuilding

- Coal

- Steel

- Hotels

- Nursing homes

- Energy generation

- They are listed on a recognised stock exchange at the time of investment.

- They are a member of a partnership with another company.

For SEIS specifically, companies must have:

- Less than £200,000 in gross assets pre-money

- No more than twenty-five employees

- Been trading fewer than two years (trading start date can be after incorporation date)

- Not previously carried out a different trade

For EIS specifically, companies must:

- Do their first EIS investment within seven years of starting trading (they can carry on raising EIS investment after seven years until a limit of £12 million is reached, with an additional limit of no more than £5 million in any one twelve-month period)

- Not control another company other than qualifying subsidiaries

- Not be controlled by another company, or have more than 50% of shares owned by another company

- Not expect to close after completing a project or series of projects

Your company and any qualifying subsidiaries must also:

- Not have gross assets worth more than £15 million before any shares are issued, and not more than £16 million immediately afterwards

- Have fewer than 250 FTE employees at the time the shares are issued

Knowledge-intensive companies

These companies have special rules for SEIS/EIS. They can raise £20 million at EIS instead of £12 million and have a ten-year fundraising window instead of seven years. They can also raise up to £10 million of investment per year, instead of £5 million.

For a company to qualify, there must be:

- Fewer than ten years since the first commercial sale

- Fewer than ten years since annual turnover went over £200,000

- Fewer than 500 full-time employees when the shares are issued

And it must meet one of these conditions:

- 15% of operating costs have been spent on innovation, research or development in one of the last three years, or 10% of operating costs in each of the three preceding years leading up to that year (if your company is fewer than three years old, this can be in the three years following investment)

- Be carrying out work to create IP and expect the majority of business to come from this within ten years (proprietary algorithms count here)

- Have 20% of employees carrying out research for at least three years from the date of investment – these employees must be in a role that requires a relevant master's or higher degree

Investors get a higher investing limit, being allowed to invest up to £2 million in their total EIS portfolio, as long as £1 million is with knowledge-intensive companies.

The rules

There are specific rules about how much you can raise and what you can do with the money.

SEIS:

- Founders can repay personal loans they've made to the company with SEIS investment.

- Raise limit is £150,000.

- If you take SEIS funding, up to £150,000 will be removed from your limits of other funding (like EIS) to match the amount of SEIS funding you received.

- Money raised must be spent within three years of share issue.

- You can't use the investment to buy shares, unless they're in a 90% subsidiary that uses the money for a qualifying business activity.

For EIS, the rules are:

- Founders *may not* repay personal loans they've made to the company with EIS investment.

- Founders can repay third-party loans with EIS if the loan was used for the purposes of the trade and it isn't linked to the investor.

In addition, the money you raise must:

- Be spent within two years of the investment, or if later, the date you started trading
- Not be used to buy all or part of another business
- Pose a risk of loss to capital for the investor
- Be used to grow or develop your business

Changes made in April 2020 apply to EIS approved funds, particularly focused on knowledge-intensive investments and timing of investments.

What it means for investors

There's a reason that 80% of UK angel investments are made through the SEIS and EIS schemes – the tax reliefs available to investors are fantastic. Investors get initial income-tax relief on a percentage of the amount invested, plus some capital gains exemptions/deferrals. They can also claim further tax relief if the business performs badly.

The rules around spending the money you raise within a certain timeframe can result in quite a change in a company's behaviour, as James White found out with InTouch:

'With EIS rules, you have to spend the money, so we'd gone from washing our face every month to burning cash. This was a different philosophy from a business perspective.'

Types of start-up investors

Angels

Angels are high net-worth individuals. Quite often, they're entrepreneurs themselves who have had a successful exit and now have some cash to invest in growing companies in the ecosystem. They typically invest in the earlier stages – pre-seed and seed, although with later rounds now appearing on crowdfunding platforms, angels are contributing at Series A as well.

Angels will invest anything from £1,000 up to several £100,000, depending on the project and their own circumstances. Some angels are dabblers and play more at the bottom end of the scale, while others are serious investors who put major stakes into fledgling companies.

How much someone will invest is also known as the ticket size. It can feel a bit awkward asking angels how much they invest, but it's quite acceptable to have a conversation about what ticket size they like to invest at. You're not asking how much money they have in their wallet, just how much they like to invest per transaction.

Chris Adelsbach is an example of the full-time end of the angel investing spectrum. Having personally invested in fifty-seven companies in the last five years, as well as another fifty through his work as a Techstars managing director, he doesn't just supply investment, but also mentorship and connections to all his portfolio companies:

> 'I make it my business to ensure that portfolio companies speak to and help one another. Angel investing has network effects, and one of the best networks is founders helping founders. I try to make this happen.'

Angels who put in significant investment may expect a seat on the board, as David Horne explains:

> 'They will get much more involved in what's going on in the business strategy, making sure the board meetings are happening, governance is in place and that you're executing on what you said you were going to do. They've put their money in and they want to see that it's being put to good use.'

Angels don't generally have their own legal teams on tap in the way that VCs do, so sometimes they can be reluctant to be the lead investor in a round because of the burden it places on them. This is something Deborah Lygonis has experienced:

'They'll say, "Yes, it's really interesting. Not really got time to do my due diligence at the moment, but if somebody else does it, let me know." Basically, they're all waiting for someone else to put their hand up to say, "Yes, we'll do it", and then they want to be part of it as well.'

Lots of angels belong to networks, like the UK Business Angels Association or the UK Angel Investment Network, which is useful as it provides a central point for accessing them. Others work as individuals and you have to find them through your own personal network.

Incubators and accelerators

Incubators and accelerators are programmes run for the development of start-ups. They're usually funded either by government or through corporate sponsorship.

The stages incubators and accelerators invest at vary massively – big government programmes like Tech Nation go from early to late stage, while some programmes (particularly those that term themselves 'incubators') only focus on the earliest stages of getting a start-up running.

Ticket size also varies massively – some of the big ones like Techstars will invest $120,000 up front, while others treat the programme as a competition with only some of the participants winning funding at the end. Some charge for the start-up to be part of their programme – it's worth doing your research to find out where each one sits on the scale.

Incubators and accelerators typically offer access to expertise not just about running a start-up, but about trade routes and talent visas as well. Programme membership often comes with office space, mentoring and investor pitching opportunities.

Google is your friend when you want to find incubators and accelerators. You need to spend a few hours in deep research mode, and ask your network what dealings they may have had with incubators and accelerators. You'll then have to go through a formal application process, which may include a pitch event, to get a place.

Crowdfunding platforms

Crowdfunding platforms aren't investors. Instead, they facilitate your access to investors through the platform. Rather than holding funds for investment in the way that a VC does, they earn money by taking a percentage of the amount you raise – typically 6–9% in the UK.

Originally focused on pre-seed and seed stages, crowdfunding platforms now offer you the opportunity to raise from pre-seed up to the early series stages. You will typically have to raise 20–30% of your total target privately before you will be allowed on to the public side of their platforms, but you can usually do this alongside preparing for the public launch, which helps to shorten the timeline.

The change in how, and how much, companies raise on crowdfunding platforms is something Luke Lang thinks is driven by entrepreneurs' focus on community:

'When we started out back in 2011, Crowdcube was positioned for start-ups, early-stage businesses looking for seed capital. Maybe they'd done their friends and family round and this was the next step for them before going on to raise a much larger round with multiple angel investors or VC firms. But that has changed over the years – we're still standing shoulder to shoulder with entrepreneurs running start-up and early-stage businesses, but increasingly we've seen much later-stage businesses looking to raise considerably larger amounts of money than we originally planned for Crowdcube.

'In the last twelve to eighteen months, we've had ten or so businesses that have raised over £5 million, which has really transformed the types of businesses that we can help to fund and finance. I think everyone's perceptions of Crowdcube and equity crowdfunding have changed, partly driven by much later-stage businesses understanding the power and benefits of raising investment beyond just the capital through Crowdcube. Over the years, Monzo has challenged our way of doing things and how we execute crowdfunding. I remember the first time they raised with us in 2016, they raised a million pounds in 96 seconds. They were still very early stage. They had built up a sense of community, openness, transparency and wanted to bring their customers and their community with them on that journey. Therefore, working with Crowdcube formed a crucial part of their proposition as a business. Early on there was a clear indication that we are different to traditional banks, we want our customers and our communities to be part of this business, we want to be involved. And they challenged us as well, they wanted to raise a million pounds, they set a cap on the amount that people could invest at £1000 – that went against perceived wisdom. Our advice at the time, your conventional wisdom at that point, was when someone wants to put £100,000 in or £200,000 in you say thank you very much and move quickly on. Monzo went into crowdfunding thinking it's not about capital, it's not about how much we raise, it's about the number of customers that we can convert into shareholders and take on our journey with us.'

Individual investors on crowdfunding platforms can invest from around £10 upwards, dependent on the platform and the minimum ticket size set by each start-up. At the other end of the scale, single investors on crowdfunding platforms have pledged as much as £1 million on one investment. Total amounts raised on crowdfunding platforms can range from £30k to £25 million in the case of BrewDog, which broke all the records.

You won't get crowdfunding platforms joining your board. Instead, their focus is much more on coaching you through the crowdfunding process itself, with people available to guide you on putting your campaign together. That doesn't mean crowdfunding is an easy route, though, something Joe Sillett can attest to:

'I'd tell start-up founders that it's not an easy process. If they think crowdfunding is a case of just doing a couple of weeks' worth of work, creating a video and some documents, sticking them up online and hoping that they're going to raise the money, they are unlikely to succeed.

'Crowdfunding is virtually a full-time job. The moment you commit to doing a crowdfunding campaign, you've got to spend the best part of four to six weeks getting everything ready. You've got to be clear about how much money you are looking to raise and what that money will be spent on. Be aware of the fact that it is a labour-intensive process that lasts for around fifty days in private and public mode.

'You have your link on the crowdfunding site. You then start prospecting around your network of people who have said they are interested. Send them the link to raise as much money as you can in private mode before you go public and visible to everyone on the main site.

'The theory goes that if you can hit between 50% and 70% of your target from hustling behind the scenes with friends, family contacts, contacts on LinkedIn and business partners, then you're going to be in great shape when you press the button that takes you fully live on the main site. That's where other investors will clearly see that your business has excellent buy-in already.'

The main platforms offer nominee administration, which means they basically act like a lead investor on behalf of all the people who've put their money in, allowing them to track the performance of their investments without having to separately engage with the start-up itself. From a start-up founder's perspective, it saves a lot of hassle and stress, particularly in a follow-on round when you've only got to get signoff from the platform as the nominee, rather than from hundreds or potentially thousands of shareholders.

The biggest crowdfunding platforms are Crowdcube, Seedrs and SyndicateRoom for pure business equity investments. Indiegogo is the biggest platform worldwide for all types of crowdfunding. You can apply online to all of them initially.

VC funds

VC funds invest other people's money by raising it from individual investors and organisations. They take all the investment decisions, so the people the money originates from are distanced from the start-ups.

Historically, VCs didn't invest at early stage, but that has changed quite a bit in recent years. Some funds now specifically invest via EIS so that their investors get the tax relief. Each VC will tend to specialise at a certain stage or on the cusp between two stages, so it's important you know where their focus is and whether they are right for your stage.

VCs can contribute anything from low thousands to millions, again depending on their specialist focus. They'll often team up with other VCs to spread the risk, so you might get one VC as the lead investor with two or three others making up the rest of the raise.

VCs will usually place a board member with your company, arguably as much to protect their investors as to offer value to you. For those VCs operating in the early-stage space, there is increasing engagement with the businesses they invest in.

This is an approach that framed how Nic Brisbourne established Forward Partners:

> 'We knew that we weren't purely an investment business. Rather, we were an entrepreneur services business. When I was setting up Forward Partners, I examined what "entrepreneur services" meant for pre-seed and seed-stage businesses. Founders would mention that while they needed all the things a VC can offer – funding, strategic advice and good contacts – their burning problems were operational. They needed answers to questions such as "How do I build my website? What do I put in the product? How do I find customers?" so we decided to work under the applied VC model, offering value-add services to our portfolio and building a much better service for our founders.

> 'It's a win-win. We offer a superior service, which enables us to win the best deals. Our

portfolio companies grow faster as a result of our help, meaning founders are happy and hitting their targets, and our investors are incentivised to invest more into the fund. We've been operating like this for six years now.'

In the UK, the highest concentration of funds is in London, but there are increasing pockets appearing around the other major cities. Some VCs will accept a deck by email, some won't, but for all of them, a better bet is a direct referral from someone they know. Increasingly, VCs are sending scouts out to start-up events, although it's obviously pot luck who they will meet.

CVCs

CVCs come from large corporates that have decided to delve into the start-up world, using it as a way of keeping a finger on the pulse. They aim to get in early as strategic investors on products that they could either use or annex to their own products. Many household names such as Orange, BP, Santander, Sky and Barclays have CVC arms.

Usually investing from seed upwards, CVCs want to see evidence of a usable product and some traction. We may know that CVCs have deep pockets, but often they're reluctant to reveal their ticket sizes.

A good CVC will, on top of their cash investment, offer start-ups expertise and potentially access to regulators and data from their own businesses, which will help to further improve the start-up's product. But there can be issues in terms of dealing with CVC goliaths, lack of speed being the most-cited problem.

Chris Adelsbach shares his thoughts on how banking CVCs need to act:

'The banks that become good partners with start-ups will have a competitive advantage because innovation doesn't totally come from within one organisation. You can't buy 100% of all the companies that you like; you have to be a good partner. If you are a partner that doesn't engage well with start-ups and you are being slow and destructive, you will get a reputation for that and will be the last partner start-up founders speak to.

'When I speak to banks' CVCs, I advise them to be good actors. They clearly can't say yes to every start-up they meet, but they must at least have an efficient process so people know whether they have a chance for collaboration. Don't drag the ass out of the process.

'CVCs also need to ensure that they don't use start-ups as a cheap form of consulting. If they do, word gets out and start-up founders – real innovators – are less inclined to partner with them. Then they'll be in real trouble.'

Russell Fisher agrees:

'The worst thing we at Nationwide could do is give a slow no. That's just awful, it's disrespectful, and frankly, decisions aren't made like that. Most people make decisions far quicker than that.

'If you're not sure, be honest and say so. Let's not waste time. Say where your concerns are, and if the founder can come back to you on that, that's cool.

'And it's a two-way street because they might not like you, which is fine. At Nationwide, we've had situations where we weren't the right fit for the start-up and we'd rather know that up front.'

For start-ups and CVCs alike, it can be hard to draw the line between investing and sales, which is where some of the delay in the process can come from. The best CVCs invest completely separately of sales, and if the start-up matures as they hope, they will then look at whether it's possible to create a sales relationship as well. At the investment stage, the start-up often isn't ready to enter into a sales relationship with a big company.

Some CVCs run their own programmes and have application forms available online, others sponsor accelerators or incubators and can choose to invest in the programme participants. The third option is to create a full venturing arm that will act like a VC – something Nationwide has done, as Russell Fisher describes:

> 'What we're trying to do with venturing is explore "things that are going to be things" in a three- to five-year timeframe. We're working with start-up founders to get access to the people who are thinking about the problem. And then we want to partner them up with people in the building society so we can understand the problem, work together, and hopefully co-develop and co-learn things.
>
> 'Lots of people say CVCs talk a great talk, but never deliver anything. That's a huge spur for us.'

Family offices

Family offices are organisations set up to manage the wealth and assets of ultra-high net-worth families, as well as establishing and managing charitable funds on their behalf. They also carry out lifestyle-management tasks, even down to schooling applications and arranging care options for elderly family members. As part of their role, they can manage entire investment funds on behalf of a family or multiple families. They may choose to invest directly in particular companies, or in funding rounds for start-ups with other investors. Family offices are not regulated like banks and generally keep a low profile.

Some, like the Holdun Family Office in Canada, are so interested in fintechs, they set up their own accelerators, while others will sit more happily in the later stages. Each family office has its own characteristics and will have interest in particular types of start-ups. Waymade Capital, the family office of Vijay and Bhikhu Patel, invests in pharma because of the family's experience in that area, whereas LSG Holdings focuses on B2C start-ups in particular.

Family offices' ticket size ranges from thousands to millions. Like CVCs, they have deep pockets for the right projects. What they offer depends on the characteristics of the family office. Some offer lots of support on top of the money, others none. Family offices generally take more of a long-term view than VCs, so if you've got a potentially long exit plan, this could be a good route.

Family offices don't tend to hang out at events in the way that VCs do. Using Google to find an appropriate target and your personal network to generate a direct referral is probably the best route to finding them.

Creating a raise strategy

This is a pivotal point in your raise journey – you've worked through vision, structure and scalability, and market. You've dug into your numbers and considered what types of investors might suit your business. Now it's time to pull all of that together into a raise strategy, so you're absolutely clear on what a good raise looks like for you.

In this section, we'll cover the seven elements you need to build a great raise strategy:

Research	Build relationships	Prepare the raise story
Investor profiling	Term sheet	Get help	Structure your raise

Before we start, Heather McDonald has some great advice which applies to the whole of your raise:

> 'Probably my biggest bit of advice is to be well organised. Be detail orientated. Take advice wherever you can get it, because it's extremely hard, so be mentally prepared and don't shy away from help.

> 'Be open to anybody who comes along because you never know who knows who. You never know what experience somebody can bring to the table. If you're doing a raise, have the

right conversations, be open to everything and respond as fast as possible.'

Element 1: Investor profiling

The investors you take on now will be with you for several years, minimum, so it's worth getting the right ones. When you're working out who your ideal investor would be, think about the ticket size you're looking for and whether you need them to bring specific expertise or connections to the table. If you're going to bring an investor on board, it makes sense to get more than just their money, as Ed Stephens shares:

'I would always start with somebody who can add strategic value or connections. They will help build the story that you tell other investors and serve as social proof for your concept.'

It's also about finding someone who will be totally on board with what you're wanting to achieve. Nic Brisbourne says:

'I would look for someone who I get on well with, who buys into the vision for my business and aligns with my thinking.'

Another thing to consider is whether you've got skin in the game (ie you have invested money yourself). Some investors won't touch a start-up if the founder doesn't stand to lose money if it all goes wrong. If for some reason you've been unable to put any cash in your business, only sweat equity (you working for free), you'll need to look specifically for investors who will consider that approach. Finally, you want an investor who knows about your area, but hasn't invested in a close competitor.

Element 2: Research

This takes a whole lot of work. Once you know what your ideal investor looks like, you've got to find them. Aim for a fairly short list of people – too often I see start-up founders contacting hundreds of people with no real plan, which is a terrible use of time.

Jonathan Lerner agrees:

'Founders spread the net far too wide. I see them reaching out to every single person in the industry, and they don't need to do that.

'You should be able to write a shortlist of five to ten investors, and then do a damn good job of pitching to those. Frankly, it's true there is probably an investor for everything some-where, but you may have to knock on lots of doors, and you may want to change your strategy if all ten on your shortlist say no. But ten should be enough for you to get some good quality feedback on either why it's not work-ing so you can refine your search, or what they don't like about your business so you can refine the model.'

When you're researching, particularly early-stage VCs, see who goes on to invest in their picks afterwards. If it looks like the same later-stage VCs each time, they've probably got relationships that mean they actively channel deal flow. By having them as investors, you get not just cash, but also a good potential ladder to the next step.

You can do research using databases like Crunchbase, Dealroom or PitchBook. If you're only doing a one-off search, you can often get a free trial membership, or you can go to the British Library, or possibly a more local library, and see if you can gain access there.

Vanessa Tierney found investors for Abodoo through three distinct routes:

'The success that I had was tracking entrepreneurs who had had successful exits in the previous three months, and then making a direct approach, knowing that they'd just made an exit or done an acquisition. That was the first approach and it worked for our first investor, who was a big one.

'The second and third investors happened to be in the audience at strategic events. Even though we weren't doing an investment pitch, we were doing a pitch on the business and they liked what they heard.

'The third route is to look for entrepreneurs or investors in the world of smart working who have co-working offices or are investing in technology ready to roll out more flexible working. They've got the space and they can see that smart working is growing exponentially.'

Finally, remember to look at your own network – who do you know, and who do *they* know? Rick Rowan did the whole of his first raise through his own contacts:

'I used my network. I already had history in the healthcare industry, so I got on the phone and started emailing, saying, "I have this idea. This is what I want to do. Are you open to having a chat about it?" As I have a pretty good reputation in the network, I got a couple of meetings and it quickly became obvious who had the capacity to potentially do something and who didn't. I then homed in on the ones that did.'

Once you've identified a list of potential investors, do your due diligence on them. Who else do they invest in? Do their values and business approach match well with yours? A good approach, if the investor runs a company, can be to look their company up on Glassdoor. What do people say about them there? Look at their social media accounts – does anything jar?

Deborah Lygonis says doing due diligence is vital to make sure you don't waste your time:

'Make sure you do your homework so that you know who you're meeting, what they have invested in before and what level they usually invest in. Otherwise, you'll waste so much time meeting the wrong people.

'Once you get the meeting, make sure that you're not intimidated by the investors. It is a two-way transaction – without you, they're not going to get richer. It's really important for start-up founders to remember that, otherwise it can feel like you're on the back foot.'

Not doing your due diligence to make sure an investor is a good fit can have negative consequences, as Elle Berrett shares:

'Founders need to know who these people are. You need to do your due diligence on the investors themselves, who might not be the right fit for your business.

'Look at their background, look at their experience, look where they've previously invested.

That's really important. I've known a situation where investment was obtained, but the relationship broke down completely because it wasn't working for either party. The dynamic wasn't there; it fell apart and got personal, and it just didn't work out. A real shame.'

Element 3: Term sheet

Even if you're going for VC investment, where the investor would generally expect to provide the term sheet, it's good practice for you to put one together yourself. The act of preparing it will help you to iron out the kinks in what you're looking for from a commercial perspective, and if you're targeting angels, then you'll probably need to provide the term sheet yourself anyway.

We will cover what the term sheet is in the 'Legal process' section of Chapter 12.

Element 4: Build relationships

The most important thing to remember about this step is this:

If you ask for money, you get advice. If you ask for advice, you get money.

People invest in people they know, so you often need to do some relationship building first, rather than steaming straight in, asking for cash. You also need to factor in getting referrals. A direct introduction from someone you know to a potential investor is 1,000 times more likely to be successful than a cold email intro.

Nic Brisbourne shares the number of approaches Forward Partners gets in a year and which ones he views as the highest quality:

'We had just over 4,000 approaches in 2018, and 2019 was even bigger. They come in through two main channels: referrals from people we know and direct outreach via our website. In comparison to the direct outreach, we get fewer referrals, but all of them are of a much higher quality.'

Some VCs offer office hours where they set aside time to give advice to start-ups for free. Georgie Hazell suggests you make the most of these:

'VC office hours can be a great way of building relationships even before you're ready to raise capital. Afterwards, keep the contacts you met in the loop with your progress with quarterly update newsletters.'

The important thing about building relationships is that you need to stay in touch, as Chris Adelsbach explains:

'People are rotten with introductions. Most of us don't have personal CRMs, we don't track who we meet and how we can help one another in the future. Start-up founders are no different, with many doing a poor job of keeping their stakeholders up to speed.

'For instance, founders can improve how they raise capital by simply ensuring they stay top of mind with investors. When a founder first meets a VC, most VCs will not invest (wouldn't it be nice if they did?), but they almost always want to stay in touch. At this point, the conversation generally ends, but it shouldn't.

'What the founder needs to be asking is, "What metrics would you like to see for me to be considered for investment?" and if the investor would like periodic updates. Most investors will say yes to additional data to help them make a decision, but you have to be disciplined about this and get updates out every month and every quarter, even if the news isn't great. Investors appreciate communication. They know things aren't going to go in a straight line, but they can't actually create that line if you don't give them data points to hang their assumptions on. You have to keep yourself front of mind.'

It isn't just you who can do relationship building. Ed Stephens suggests you use your existing investors and board members, if you have them:

'Go for broke and start with ideal investors. A way to lure them in might be a strong advisory panel and/or a highly experienced chairman. Investors ultimately are excited to invest in start-ups, but they like security. The people around you who will be helping to advise how money is spent add security.'

A great way to get good referrals in to investors is through other start-ups they've already invested in. In your research, take note of where they've invested and ask the founders if they could give you some advice on the raise process and how they found their investors. If the founder likes the sound of your company and your product or service, they may well offer to introduce you.

If you can't find a connection who can introduce you to an investor, then you need to contact them in a way that helps you stand out from the crowd. Dan Bowyer has some suggestions:

'Sometimes I would have meetings with people because they have done something different or interesting, or they have reached out in a new way. As much as you may like to be data driven, investors are human beings who want something to touch them emotionally, as well as the numbers making sense.

'Don't take no for an answer. I really like it when people hassle me and say, "I know this is what you do and I know that we are right for you, so meet me for a cup of tea. Let's go, I want to show you some stuff."'

Ideally you will build relationships continuously, which you can then leverage when it comes to a raise. Vanessa Tierney agrees:

'I've done a lot of pre-pitching to VCs for our series A in the future, so my relationship building is started with them.'

Element 5: Get help

When you're putting together a raise, having the right advisors and expertise around you is vital. It's something I referred to right back in Chapter 1, but now you're on the brink and you need to make a decision.

For many start-up founders, the finances and the details of commercial points are the 'scary bit'. At

Spark! we partner with Evoke Management, a company that will supply founders with a part-time FD throughout their raise and beyond – a highly experienced pair of hands that can add real value to your raise.

Heather McDonald found WooHa Brewing just didn't have the breadth of experience when it came to the marketing and PR needed for a crowdfunding round:

> 'We hired a PR company, which made a huge difference with the amount of PR that we're getting, the amount of press that we're getting, the social that's out there. And the activity on the Crowdcube page itself has been really good. It's kept us in the forefront of people's minds.'

Element 6: Prepare the raise story

For every raise you do, you need a clear story to go with it. This isn't about making things up – far from it – but you need to be able to communicate a few things to your potential investors:

- Where you fit in the ecosystem
- What raising money will enable you to do
- Key things that are happening in your business

Where you fit in the ecosystem. For some companies, it's obvious where they fit, but if you are doing something completely new, it can be hard for investors to get their heads around it. Deborah Lygonis, whose start-up Friendbase sits across gaming, education and culture, has found it can be tricky if you don't fit into a certain pigeonhole:

> 'Investors have their criteria and they need to evaluate you against the criteria they've set. If you can't be defined, they just don't know what to look at.'

Deborah isn't the only one to have experienced this. Mark Abbott has found the same at Supermoney, which uses Blockchain:

> 'The more complex the solution is, the more likely it is that investors don't have anyone within their team to understand it. Then they just say, "No, not interested." That has been the biggest problem.'

Everything was new once, but people are naturally wary of what they don't understand. James White recalls the difficulties around raising money for online software when cloud was still in its infancy:

> 'Being able to explain online software at that time was hard. People now wouldn't worry about a cloud-based app, but in 2012/13,

people were still talking about desktop software. That made them concerned around security and that side of things.'

From an investor perspective, Ed Stephens says if you don't know the area the start-up falls in, it's important to let the facts do the talking:

'Facts speak, so if something is revenue generating, is winning clients and proving itself out in the market to some degree, you have got to take it on its performance. It's worth exploring how it's achieving this as its real-world validation.

Sometimes it might be a company where you don't personally see the value, but you can remove yourself from the concept and say "it's just doing well. I can evaluate it on that basis." But a word of caution with this is spotting venture bloat, when a company's revenue is being manipulated by driving money through the marketing channels. Companies doing this can post good revenues, but are compromised on cash-flow and EBITDA.'

What raising money will enable you to do. Investors – naturally – want to know what their money will be spent on, so it's important to be able to tell the story of what outcomes you hope to achieve. Heather McDonald shares:

'Investors want to invest in what will grow the business. Their money needs to actually be driving the valuation of the company.

'The first raise we did on Crowdcube was for a specific thing: to grow our capacity. The message going out was, "WooHa could sell a lot more beer if we were able to package it better." From that standpoint, we went in with a specific mission for a specific piece of equipment.'

Key things that are happening in your business. As part of your raise story, make sure that you have achievements to share and can clearly show progression towards your vision. Rather than passively summarising what you've done, actively get things in place that will impress potential investors.

This is something Heather McDonald made a real point of:

'We did a few key things prior to the raise. There was some change in staff. We brought on high-profile employees to beef up the management team, and we've now got the history with our chairman as well. We made sure we got contracts in place so that we would have some exciting things to speak about.

'For this raise, what's created a lot of momentum is that there's an extremely clear path on how we'll get from where we are to where we want to go. And that's the difference between this and our first raise: a clear strategic goal. Everything that we do – everything in our business plan, including our financial trajectories – is all aligned completely with that strategic goal, so when I speak to investors now, they know that I know where I'm going and that everybody is behind me, and that we have a well-articulated plan for delivering. It's made a big difference.'

Joe Sillett took an equally professional approach to The Funky Appliance Company's raise:

'Make sure that the story you deliver to your investors is what they would like to hear. What have you done with the money that you got in round two, round one? Has the money been spent carefully and wisely? Where is the business now? Is the business ready to tell the story that it needs to tell? Why do you need this next round of money? Where will this money be invested?

'We've spent quite a lot of time this year working on a funky kettle and a funky toaster. They have now been designed and are ready, but they will need separate investment to take the business up on to a multi-product level. That's why we're doing a series A funding round.'

Element 7: Structure your raise

The final step in creating your raise strategy is thinking about how you structure the raise itself. That means how many different types of investment you'll seek, how many investors you want, how much equity to give away and the timeline for the raise.

Investment often doesn't all come from one source. If you're crowdfunding, for instance, you may raise the initial amount with angels, and then go to the crowd, or you may end up with a family office as a lead investor with a couple of VCs joining in as well. You may even raise part of the round through a business grant, so it's worth thinking about what money you want to get from where.

But too many investors isn't great. Scrappy cap tables, too many opinions, or people who've only put in a minimal amount and aren't really engaged with you as a company don't look good. For this reason, Deborah Lygonis has targeted investors with capacity to absorb the whole round:

'We have approached the kind of organisations that are quite capable of taking the whole round themselves. That would be ideal, because then they will be more engaged and probably have a seat on the board. They will be more active as well in promoting us into their networks.'

Back to the Goldilocks theme, too few investors may not be 'just right' either, as Ed Stephens explains:

> 'Some people say something like, "I want to raise £300k and I want it from three investors", but I wouldn't do that at the expense of taking on a really amazing investor for £25k, £20k, £15k who makes the other £280k really easy to raise. If you have four of those people, you've raised up to £100k, and if they are happy with you, in a future round they would probably double up. Then you would immediately get another £100k, whereas if you just get one investor with £100k and they're then maxed out or have too much control, you are in trouble.
>
> 'Lots of people get their series A round delayed as they enter into diligence phases with funds. At that point, they have to do bridge rounds. The internal marketing of these rounds is important as existing investors will often prop you up and keep you solvent.'

Calculating how much equity you're willing to exchange for funding is about weighing up your valuation, how much money you need to raise and how much control you're happy to give up. If you need to raise £250k and your valuation is £1 million, that would mean giving up 25% of equity. A general rule of thumb at early stage is that investors will be looking for a 10–20% stake in the company. Be careful of giving more than that away – it might mean you're trying to raise too much on too low a valuation.

Raises can drag on and on if you're not careful. The best approach is to plan them like a project with a set end date that you can drive towards. Make sure you won't be trying to finalise deals during school holidays or any major festivals, and then be prepared to push hard to meet that timeline.

This is a strategy that Vanessa Tierney follows:

> 'The tip I got after a year or two was to set a deadline date for investment, because it can roll on and on and on and people can take their time. Have a term sheet ready to send as soon as an investor's waiting, send it within the hour and use e-signature. Term sheet signed, it's then cash. You can look after share certificates later on, but it's worth striking while the iron is hot.'

That brings us to the end of the fifth step on the Investor Ready Roadmap, and we've covered a lot. We've looked at the SEIS and EIS, at the different types of investors out there, and worked through creating a raise strategy, but the key things I would like you to take from this chapter are:

- An understanding of which investors are right for you and your company – don't waste time talking to ones who aren't right

- A clear investment strategy which will ultimately save you time and make sure you don't miss anything vital

The final step on the roadmap is pitch, which is all about how you communicate everything you've worked on to potential investors.

ELEVEN

Step Six – Pitch

This is the culmination of the whole preparation process. In this chapter, we'll be covering not just the pitch itself, but all the elements around it:

- The golden rules

- The data funnel

- Business plan

- Pitch deck

- One-pager

- Data rooms

- Video

- Product demos

- Verbal pitch

- Practise!

Before we dive into the detail, this guidance from Luke Lang is useful to take with you through the whole chapter:

> 'Businesses that really stand out to me are those that treat the raise seriously. The founder recognises that this is an exercise in fundraising, but it's also at heart an exercise in marketing and communications.

> 'You've got a proposition, which is your business, your products, your services, your team, the market opportunity, and you want to present that proposition, but you need to communicate it effectively to different audiences, different customers and different people. Your customers will be different to your existing shareholders, to potential angel investors. Founders who appreciate and understand that and approach it in a professional manner spend time thinking about how they're going to communicate their business rather than their product.

> 'That's the kind of change in gear that you need to make. You're not just promoting and selling your product; you're promoting and selling your business. That's clearly your

products and services, but it's also your team, your market opportunity, the mission that you're on and the vision you have for a better world.'

The golden rules

Whether you're working on your deck, a verbal pitch or a video, these are the golden rules of pitching to live by:

- Get the level of detail right. Too much and it dilutes your message, making it hard to pick out the key points.

- Don't bore people. Pitches are about delivering enough information to create positive energy and interest. When you tip over into providing too much information, you push people towards boredom and apathy, which is not what you want.

- Find a way to stand out. There are thousands of other start-ups out there competing for attention.

- Tailor your pitch to your audience. This shows you're interested in the specific investor you're addressing.

- Know your numbers inside out. You're talking to a mixture of lawyers, accountants, tax specialists, fund managers, successful entrepreneurs and strategists (no pressure!).

- You *must* be able to back up any claims you make. Scepticism is strong and everything you claim will be checked. Claims that don't stand up will seriously damage your credibility.

- Use credible reports to back up what you're saying.

- Eat your own dog food. If there's a way to use your own product in your pitch that isn't contrived, make sure you do so.

- Your company's culture and brand must come through in your pitch. The words you use, the visuals you use – everything must contribute to reinforcing them.

- Don't use initials and acronyms – nobody wants to be made to feel stupid.

Russell Fisher explains what he expects:

'Provide decent data, data that an investor will recognise. There's no point in citing a report that nobody's ever heard of from somebody who's not credible.'

The data funnel

Before we get into the separate elements of your pitch materials, let's talk about the data funnel. At the widest point is the most detail, and at the narrowest point, the least detail – I'm sure you get the drift.

The important thing to bear in mind is consistency throughout the funnel. From the data room all the way down to a one-pager, everything must say the same thing; nothing must be different. When you're preparing materials and iterating fast, it's easy to add something in one place that you don't mention elsewhere. This will trip you up, and whether that's during a pitch or due diligence, it will be painful. Remember from the data room down, everything is a distillation of the layer above and must be consistent.

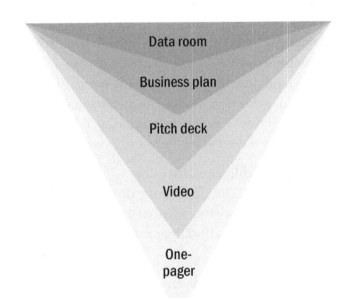

When preparing materials, I find it's best to start with the business plan and get that right, then do the pitch deck, the data room, and finally one-pagers and videos. This is a different order to the funnel because your business plan dictates everything else that you need. You can't know what you should be sharing in your data room until you have a business plan, and you can't produce a pitch deck either, if you don't first have a plan.

Business plan

Your business plan gets used at three points:

- When you're in second-stage discussion with an investor. They've seen your deck and/or your pitch, and now they want to know more. Ask them to sign a non-disclosure agreement before you hand over your business plan, as it will contain confidential business information.

- During due diligence. Investors will refer to the business plan a lot during due diligence to check what you've said and whether you have the documentation to back that up.

- After you've raised. You'll need it yourself after you've raised to make sure that as you deliver on your strategy, you hit all the points you promised.

Your business plan is an aggregation of everything you've worked on so far. It should be around thirty to thirty-five pages in length, well laid out with a contents page and page numbering. Making your documents easy to use is a small thing investors will appreciate.

When it comes to your business plan, Joe Sillett recommends you provide as much insight as possible:

'It's all about the planning and the detail of the planning. Over-deliver on detail rather than just summarise. The more insight you can provide to the investor who's looking at the plan – the numbers, the team behind it – the better. At the end of the day, you are educating people about the opportunity and what the opportunity may or may not become in the future. Investors like detail and a clear plan.'

As you pull your plan together and see it 'in the round' for the first time, Heather McDonald says it's a great time to challenge what you've written:

'Question everything you put together in a model. Look at it and say, "OK, why are we doing this? Why are we hiring that person? Why are we targeting this growth? Why do we think that we're going to be doing 18% of our turnover from Europe in year three? Why did we put that there?" You need to understand all the whys behind your model.'

Your business plan needs to tell the whole story of your business in detail. Start with an executive summary, and then include (the order is not prescribed, you need to work out the right flow for your company):

- Company summary (incorporation details, time since incorporation, how the company is structured, awards)

- Company values

- Team

- The problem – use graphs and images to prove how bad the problem is

- The market opportunity

- Mission and passion – what change you want to bring and why

- The solution – images, key features, benefits, the secret sauce (what makes you different and better than your competitors)

- Product roadmap

- Revenue model

- Achievements so far

- Company roadmap

- Competitors and barriers to market entry

- What IP you have and how you've protected it

- Financials – detailed projections, past performance

- What the raise will be spent on, prior raises, SEIS/EIS qualification

- Ideal investor profile and exit

- Team

- Go-to-market strategy

- Operations and logistics

- Assets

- Technology

- Benchmark details

- Risk analysis

Dan Bowyer says:

> 'Don't make me work for it. What is the thing, what is the value of it? Sometimes that is really boring – your product could just be paperclips, but it's how you make the paperclips and the market that you sell them into that is the real magic sauce.'

Pitch deck

The hardest thing about pitch decks is how short they need to be – but it's also the best thing. I recommend ten to fifteen slides maximum. Condensing everything you want people to know into that small amount of slides can seem impossible, but it's actually a great exercise that forces you to think about all the details of your company and how you present them to others.

The other key thing to remember is that your pitch deck is a visual document, intended for summary and presentation only. You'll have other documents which give far more detail for potential investors, so your pitch deck only needs about ten words per slide as an average. Full sentences – or worse, paragraphs – have no place in your deck.

Ed Stephens says it's worth taking real care when putting your pitch deck together:

> 'Early signs of care and attention matter. A really nicely put-together pitch deck seems obvious, but it's easy to think, "Whatever, it's just communication of information." Think of it like when you get customer complaints and go the extra mile to attend to their needs and address their issues diligently. Make things look presentable and nice. It makes a difference.'

Depending on what investment route you take, you may use your pitch deck in a number of ways:

- As slides when presenting your pitch

- As a deck that you can email to someone or print out for them to read

- As a downloadable document on a crowdfunding platform for potential investors to view

The crowdfunding point is an interesting one, because it reminds you that your audience for a pitch deck could be anyone. That's why it shouldn't contain detailed or confidential information that you wouldn't want competitors to see.

Vanessa Tierney had to come up with the right balance of sharing enough information to hook people without giving too much away about Abodoo:

'When it came to the crowdfunding, it was interesting. This is public information – anyone can go on and request your deck, and you can end up approving everybody.

'We didn't want to give everything away, so we added just enough for potential investors to realise that we had a clear vision and strategy and how we were going to execute, without the minute detail. Our competitor could have been accessing the information – that's the reality.'

Here's another useful bit of advice from Luke Lang (he's good at this!):

'Outline your business in a clear and coherent manner. Use plain English to explain what you're doing, making it clear and concise and compelling for individuals.'

Pitch decks are usually produced in PowerPoint, and then pdf form before you send them anywhere. This means no one can change the document easily. Also, by the time you've added lots of images in, the file size can be massive. Remember, this is a distillation of the business plan, so many things will be the same, but communicated more simply.

Don't waste your pitch deck's front cover; use it to convey a key message, either about your product or about what you want. Include company name, logo and founder contact details, including mobile phone numbers. A simple image and a powerful tagline are ideal.

It's important your front cover conveys your brand, which doesn't just mean colours and typefaces, but also culture. A children's entertainment company's front cover, for instance, should convey how bright, happy and energetic it is, while a cyber-security company should portray safety and security. Your front cover really helps set the scene for what's inside.

Once you have your front cover right, the slides need to cover:

- Slide 1: The problem
- Slide 2: Market opportunity
- Slide 3: Mission and passion
- Slides 4–6: The solution – images, key features, benefits, the secret sauce
- Slide 7: Revenue model
- Slide 8: Achievements so far
- Slide 9: Roadmap
- Slide 10: Competitors
- Slide 11: Financials
- Slide 12: What the raise will be spent on, prior raises, SEIS/EIS qualification
- Slide 13: Ideal investor profile and exit
- Slide 14: Team

Depending on what you're using the deck for, you could change the order of a couple of the slides. If you're presenting face-to-face, I'd put the team slide first, because people want to know the credibility of the people in front of them. If you're sending your deck to someone to read, I'd put that at the back and let them get hooked by the problem and the solution first.

Once you've prepared the deck, get someone who has never read it before to review it. One of her best plans, says Vanessa Tierney, was:

> 'Using other entrepreneurs to look at the deck that we'd put together to see if it was hitting the mark and asking them to be critical, then revising that deck probably 100 times before saying, "OK, it's good enough".'

One-pager

Some VCs like a one-pager and some angel investment platforms request one too. Plus, it's a great handout to give to anyone you meet who may be interested in your company.

The aim with a one-pager is not to cram as many words into it as possible. Instead, it's a distillation of your pitch deck in visual form. At Spark! we tend to focus on four things: problem, solution, credibility (in this instance, credibility includes founder, traction, awards and notable PR) and how much money a business needs (including whether there's advance assurance for SEIS/EIS). A one-pager needs to be visually engaging. Someone looking at it needs to be able to quickly understand what it is you do.

Data rooms

Firstly, a data room isn't actually a room (it obviously was at some point in the past, before computers made the room redundant). It's a secure storage location in the cloud where you deposit all the information you need to share with investors so that they can access it. You can do it simply with a Dropbox that you grant access to, or you can use a specific tool that has access management and tracking, like iDeals or SecureDocs.

A common refrain from early-stage start-up founders is 'We won't need a data room, we're so early we haven't got anything to put in it.' Wrong. Even a very early-stage company will have plenty to add. Preparing the data room while you're preparing your pitch deck and business plan is good practice – it saves a mad scramble when an investor asks a question and it looks professional.

This is an approach Russell Fisher is a fan of:

'Getting a good data room together is time well spent. It shows you're investor ready, and that's the point. That gives investors comfort. If a business has a data room, it sounds like the founder knows what they're doing. They're serious about the round.'

Data rooms are used during the due diligence exercise – 90% of what investors will ask in Due Diligence Questions (DDQ) can be predicted. They're the same for everyone, which means you can prepare your data room based on that 90%.

There are nine key areas of data you'll need to put in your data room:

- Company overview
- Market (this will include market analysis and any market data you have)
- Customers and suppliers (contracts, lists of suppliers, sales literature all go here)
- Operations (everything from insurance details to IT design)
- Legal (shares, licences, trademark registrations)
- Finance and tax (financial statements, debtors, creditors etc)
- Planning (business plans and planned capital expenses)
- Reporting
- HR (employment contracts, employee handbooks etc)

The full list is too long to share here, so visit www.spark-consulting.co.uk/are-you-investor-ready and complete the 'Are You Investor Ready?' scorecard. We'll then send you a copy of the Spark! Due Diligence Checklist, which has over 120 items on it.

Video

A good pitch video can be used in a multitude of ways – put it on the home page of your website, put it out on social media, use it for your crowdfunding campaign. Sometimes VCs and CVCs will request a video to share with their investment board, as Russell Fisher explains:

'At Nationwide, one of the challenges when we go to our advisory board is we don't want to bring the start-up founders with us to stand up for five minutes in a dragon's den environment. Instead, we now ask them to do a little video.

'It's wonderful to see the creativity and how well some people treat it, and how badly others do. It's been wonderful and terrible in equal measure. Because it's so hard for us to talk with the passion the founders have, the video can speak a lot about the start-up and how much thought the founder has given to their audience and what they should be saying to them.'

Video is about connecting as human beings. This isn't the time to screen-share your pitch deck and talk over it. If people want to see video, they want to see you – your passion, your knowledge and your customers if possible. They want to see your belief in the future, that you can be the change that will make the difference. It's the time to proudly show off your product, to talk about the change it's made in people's lives already, about how that made you feel.

Give a great call to action at the end. Let investors know how much money you need and what it will help you achieve – and remember to mention your SEIS/EIS assurance. Oh, and keep it under three to four minutes – see earlier point about boredom...

Product demos

If there's one law of product demos, it's that your product will go wrong on the day. I was once supposed to be demoing a new website to a group of about thirty businesspeople when the building lost all internet signal and I couldn't access it. I'd love to say I had cleverly printed off posters of the website, but sadly, no.

What I did have in my arsenal was I knew the damn site like the back of my hand, so I drew it on flip charts, with all the buttons and links, and demoed it anyway. I got a standing ovation at the end, but it was possibly the most stressful presentation of my life!

The moral of the story is to have a triple backup plan every time. Demo live if you can, but if that doesn't work, have screenshots saved in a PowerPoint deck that you can use instead. If your laptop doesn't work, have paper copies on stand-by. If it's a physical product, always take two with you if you can, just in case one gets dropped or damaged somehow.

Remember the people watching the demo have never seen your product before. Go slowly, ask for questions before you move from one screen to another. If there's any fiddly registration process or anything that seems like a faff, do that beforehand if you can. If the point of your product is speed, say you'll do the whole process first to show how quick it is, then you'll go back and do it again more slowly, with opportunity for questions.

It's important to tailor your demos to your audience. Keep it simple as a general rule, but if there are specific technical specialists there, make sure you point out a few key technical gems to them. This is what Mark Abbott did when he demoed his Supermoney product to a group of tech specialists:

'We went through the actual real-time frames of looking on the ledger, and we gave a live demo of what happens with the code and how the tokens are created. That was powerful stuff because the tech guys made a point of saying they'd never seen this before, and they thought it was fantastic.'

Verbal pitch

When will you use this? All. The. Time. Every person you meet, you're pitching to. Every person you meet probably has a link to someone who could help you.

It doesn't mean you have to act like Smarmy Steve the Salesman (sorry Steves everywhere, but alliteration is powerful). The point of having a verbal pitch is not that you recite the damn thing in its entirety to every person you see. It's more than that.

Through creating a verbal pitch, you learn how to communicate your proposition so well that you can use parts of the pitch in a one-minute conversation, or in a three-minute presentation, or in a meeting over coffee. It's about figuring out how you are going to talk about your company in a way that is compelling and engaging.

If someone invites you for a coffee and a chat, David Horne advises:

'Make no mistake, it's not a conversation; it's a pitch. It may be happening like a conversation, but it's definitely a pitch. Particularly when you're getting into VC-type discussions where there's something scientific involved, the VC will have their expert. It's often the quiet person who sits in the corner and listens to everything, and then all of a sudden comes up with the killer question that rips everything to shreds. You have to be ready for that.'

There are some specific strategies you can use to help you in your pitch. The first one is to hook people quickly, as James White explains:

'Capture them early, excite them early. Let them know there's a big problem or a big issue that you're addressing, that you're solving.'

When you get to the end of your pitch, instead of trailing off, follow Vanessa Tierney's lead and end with a question that will help smoke out objections and hopefully close the deal:

'You can ask the question "What else can I tell you?" and you'll find out there and then if they're going to invest or what's stopping them from investing. Hopefully you can handle it or provide them with data after the fact to help close it.'

How you behave when you're pitching is also key. David Horne advises:

> 'Don't be afraid to put yourself out there. And be human. Be vulnerable because people respond to that.'

This is echoed by Jonathan Lerner:

> 'I sometimes see founders not being themselves. They over-pitch, if you like, and come across as more arrogant than people who know them would say they are. That's a huge error. You need to be "on it" in a pitch, but you need to be humble as well. I've definitely not done investments when I've liked the business, and would actually have liked the entrepreneur generically, but their pitch made me feel like I'd not be able to work with them.'

Arrogance is a trait Dan Bowyer says founders need to a degree, but not to the point where it damages their pitch:

> 'You need the CEO to be arrogant enough to sell, to stand in front of investors and clients and be fabulous, but you also need them to know when to shut up. I had a pitch where the CEO wouldn't let his co-founders speak, and that was an instant "Woah!"'

When pitching to investors, Joe Sillett says he aims for a combination of energy, enthusiasm and detailed preparation.

'Know your numbers inside out. Have a clear vision of the journey you expect to take investors on. Communicate why investors should want to be a part of your business. It should excite them and encourage an emotional connection, leaving them wanting to be involved.'

Your verbal pitch basically needs the same content as your pitch deck, but turned into a conversational tone. You don't want to say, 'And now we'll turn to slide three and review the financials'; you need to tell a story about why you started your business, how you've got to where you are now and where you're going next.

Practise!

Once you've got all your pitches prepared, the first thing to do before you take them anywhere is to step back for a couple of days. Go and do something else entirely; don't even think about them. Then look through them all again with fresh eyes to see if anything stands out as wrong.

For your pitch scripts, it's a good idea to read the whole thing through out loud and see how it sounds. You'll soon realise which bits might jar, or where a sentence is too long. Next, you need to go through the practise/feedback loop a few times before you end up in front of someone who really counts.

These are the practise/feedback loops I'd recommend you go through.

Record your verbal pitches

Use the voice recorder on your phone. Learn your pitch beforehand to the point where you're not reading from the script, and then afterwards listen back. Are you using the right words? Are you speaking clearly and coherently? Does your voice have the kind of energy you want?

You may realise at this point that you sound a bit flat – it's a common issue. For pitches, you pretty much always need to add energy in, which may feel uncomfortable to you, but it's time to step out of your comfort zone and display your passion for your product. No one is going to invest in a founder who isn't excited by their product.

For the perfectionists among you, don't get stuck in an endless loop of self-criticism. This is just the first step. Do it a few times, then move on.

Practise in front of friends, your management team or a mentor

For friends in particular, give them criteria you want them to think about while you're speaking. They may not be experienced in pitching either, so it can be helpful to tell them what good looks like. Then they can add their own personal impressions as well.

From these sessions, build up a bank of questions people ask and work out the best way to answer them. Just because someone has asked a question, it doesn't always mean you need to shoehorn that information into your pitch. If it's a big area that you've somehow missed, then of course put it in, but if it's a detail question relating to a section you've covered, leave it out of your pitch. But be prepared to answer it in full.

Pitch at a general investor event

There's a chance there may be someone at an event who could be a suitable investor for you, but it's usually a general crowd. You may get lucky, but don't pin your hopes on winning investment here. This is just another opportunity to practise and get feedback. It's also a great opportunity to get someone to video you, so you can use the footage on social media.

This brings us to the end of the Investor Ready Roadmap, and we've covered a lot. You are now equipped with everything you require to get the investment you need.

The key points to take from this final chapter of the roadmap are:

- Everything must be consistent across all materials and spoken pitches.

- Everything you say, you must be able to back up somewhere in your documentation.

- You need to be well-practised at pitching in multiple scenarios. Being confident is key.

Now it's time to have a look at what happens next.

PART THREE

BEYOND THE ROADMAP

TWELVE

What Happens Next?

You've pitched for investment. What happens now?

In this chapter, we'll cover these areas:

- Handling rejection
- The investor said yes – what next?
- The legal process
- The due diligence exercise
- Finalising the deal
- Getting back to normal
- This is day one

Handling rejection

Ouch! It's always hard to take a no, especially when you've put your heart and soul into your pitch, but if there's one thing entrepreneurship teaches you, it's resilience. No isn't the end; it's a great learning opportunity.

The first priority is to find out what triggered the no – ask for feedback there and then if the investors aren't directly volunteering it. Was it your product, your market, your team, the quality of your pitch, your and your team's behaviour? If the answer is that it was none of these, more that your business is slightly too early for the investors, ask for a referral to people who do invest at that stage.

If you really believe they're the investor for you and you think their reasons are things you can fix quickly, ask for an opportunity to come back to them maybe in a month's time when you've had a chance to re-set. If the meeting has left you feeling they aren't the investor for you, take careful note of why, review your ideal investors list and maybe tweak it, and then move forward with a better view of who you're looking for.

If the investor's no is based on things you can't fix straight away, like customer traction, treat it as a relationship you can build on and keep in touch.

The investor said yes – what next?

The first thing to do is pause. The investor may have said yes, but you haven't yet. Now that you've met them, this is the time to assess whether you really feel they will be a good investor for you.

Assuming you agree to proceed, the next step is to alert your lawyers that the deal is happening so they can start the paperwork. You then need to agree commercial terms with the investor. Your lawyer will make sure everything is done properly from a legal perspective, but it's important you negotiate the key commercial terms yourself.

Solicitor Elle Berrett explains how it can derail the process later if this isn't done properly up front:

'The start-up founders, and their instructions, that have impressed me the most are those who have negotiated and agreed all of the commercial points surrounding a raise. By commercial, I simply mean not legal points. It's really frustrating when we get down the line in a particular fundraising process, we're not far off completion, and then all of a sudden, a significant commercial point springs to light that a founder and an investor haven't talked about and agreed yet. Things like that are difficult for us as legal advisors because commercial decisions are something that founders and investors need to agree between themselves.'

The legal process

A term sheet will be issued first, either by you or by the investor, depending on what type of investor they are. The term sheet isn't a legally binding document; it's a discussion document that is used to agree all the key points before the formal documents, such as the shareholders' agreement or investment agreement, are prepared. It will include things such as the maximum share price, whether it will be straight equity investment or a convertible loan note, and any conditions the investor wants to impose. It should cover issues such as dilution of shares (how and when that happens) and whether any shares have preferential rights attached to them.

There are some key things that often crop up at this stage, which Elle feels founders need to be aware of:

'There's something called pre-emption rights that can attach to shares. A typical example would be an investor comes along, you have your investment agreement, then they request that there are pre-emption rights in the agreement. This means that if any of the existing founders want to leave the business or transfer or sell their shares, they have to offer those shares to the investor first.

'It may or may not be an issue, but pre-emption rights are worth thinking about as they give founders less flexibility to offer shares out to the public and get external shareholders coming in. Quite often, investors want to approve the process anyway if further funding is being sought or further shares issued. Ultimately, they will have some control over that element of the further raising processes.

'Often investors will want preferential rights attached to shares, which basically means that they get preferential dividend returns compared to founders who will probably hold ordinary shares. It's important to consider that. Investors will also likely want to sit on the board or have a say in how the company is run, and there may be a schedule attached to the back of an investment agreement or shareholders' agreement stipulating a load of transactional matters that relate to the company that cannot be done without the investors' consent. It could be things such as entering into a loan agreement with the bank or another third party, changing the company's articles or spending over a certain amount. Sometimes that figure is really low, which can be fairly restrictive for a founder. Ultimately, it's their business.

'Finally, be aware of the implications of warranties and indemnities that are sometimes put into the investment agreement, in which you're essentially promising that the business and affairs of your company are presented in the way that they exist. If that's not the case, further down the line, you could be sued by the investor. Just be prepared to give those if need be.'

Once you've agreed terms, the final documentation will be prepared. This will include the investment agreement or shareholders' agreement and possibly a subscription agreement, dealing with which rights will be attached to the investor's shares and the implications of that.

The company's articles of association may also need to be amended to reflect the new arrangement. It's important to make sure this gets done, otherwise there can end up being competition between the shareholder agreement and the articles of association, with uncertainty over which one rules. If you want to read through some draft examples of these documents, take a look at the British Private Equity and Venture Capital Association website (www.bvca.co.uk) for model copies that you can view and download for free.

It can be tempting to do it yourself, but if there any complexities to the deal, you'll be in a terrible situation where you won't know what you don't know, and could miss something vital. This happened to one of Elle's clients:

'I had a situation where the client prepared their own documents, and further down the line, there was a problem. There were certain things in the documentation that didn't protect the client at all, and the investor was dissatisfied. The start-up had to incur loads of costs for me to redo everything, which then had to get the subsequent approval from the investor. And the whole thing was just a shambles, wasting company money on something that should have been done right from the start.'

The due diligence exercise

Due diligence shouldn't be painful if you've prepared your data room well. The investor will send a list of due diligence questions and you will be expected to answer all of them and provide supporting documentation as well. This is a great opportunity to impress investors with fast turnaround on responses and good quality documentation.

Elle shares what works and the challenges she experiences in due diligence:

'What impresses me are founders who are really on top of all of their financials and commercials, and active in the due diligence process. They upload documents to the data room in a timely manner, and are happy and willing to provide paperwork and answers to information requested by investors quickly and in a fashion that makes sense.

'I've come across situations where investors have asked fairly straightforward questions to founders who don't know the answer or give a wishy-washy answer. And I think, "Gosh, by now, you should have this information to hand." I've seen clients who don't even know that due diligence is part of the process. And although I'm there to explain and help walk them through it, they sometimes try to cut costs by doing it themselves.

'I totally understand there are cash-flow implications and costs to the legal side of things, which we always try to keep to a minimum. But please make sure that it's done in the right way and answer the specific questions you've been asked, because otherwise it will come back to bite you and prolong the due diligence exercise.'

At Nationwide, due diligence is spread out over a longer period, as Russell Fisher explains:

'We don't start the due diligence post investment board; we've done it as we've gone
through, but it takes it a step up when we go
through to investment board. We will do technical due diligence, background checks on the
business, background checks on the founders
all beforehand as part of our process, and start
trickling out the due diligence questions so
founders know what to expect.

'We have quite an extensive list of questions.
I'm expecting them all to be answered, even
if it's just "This isn't relevant because…" We
expect founders to look at each question,
acknowledge it and respond, so the list can
look quite intimidating. But the questions are
there for a reason. All founders should have
answers to them.'

Due diligence isn't just what *you* can tell your investors. Be prepared for investors to contact your clients
as part of due diligence as well. In fact, Dan Bowyer
says this is the most important part of the exercise:

'A lot of due diligence is around speaking to
clients and prospective clients. It doesn't matter what start-up founders say, it doesn't matter what they think; it only matters what the
customer wants, does, thinks and says.'

Luke Lang feels the extent of the due diligence process can be a real shock to some people:

> 'Some business owners aren't expecting that. They're not familiar with financial promotions regulations, with all of the statements of fact on their pitch that they're going to need to provide verification notes and evidence for, which need to be third party. We can't just get a note from your grandmother saying that it's true; we need proper evidence.'

Finalising the deal

It's important to make sure that you have time blocked out for finalising the deal and are fully available, either for last-minute questions, reviewing documents with your lawyer or signing things.

Elle Berrett shares a situation where her client went AWOL during the process:

> 'The client was uncontactable. I was liaising with the investor's solicitor, we were being proactive, getting documents agreed from a legal side of things, but I could never get hold of my client. It was the final instruction, confirmation and sign off, and she was unavailable.

'I appreciate we're all busy, but this is a particularly important aspect of the business. The founder must be there, making themselves available.'

Founders aren't the only ones who go missing during the process, though, as Russell Fisher explains:

'There were thirty-five individual investors, and we expected everybody to sign on to our shareholder agreement. Because we're a CVC, we're bit more demanding on that than others may be. But one of the investors was literally up a mountain and one was on safari in Africa, so the founders couldn't get them to sign it. Meanwhile, weeks burnt away.'

Once the deals are signed, there's still some work to do. There will be board and shareholder resolutions which need to be approved and correctly filed at Companies House, and you must ensure that the share capital alterations made are also properly reported to Companies House. There are deadlines attached to filing some of this documentation, so make sure you know what those are.

Getting back to normal

Once the deal is done, it's tempting to feel that you can get back to normal now, but the reality is you have a new normal – one that requires board meetings, shareholder reporting, investor relations, keeping your books immaculate all the time in case investors ask to see them. You may have additional obligations set out in the investment agreements that you need to adhere to as well. And of course, now you've got the money, you've got to do something with it.

James White remembers 'the morning after':

> 'I looked at the bank account and the solicitors had transferred the funds. I remember thinking, "Wow, there's a lot of money in there" and staring a bit goggle eyed at it. For a long time, I had been bootstrapping it, but now the business had a lot of money. What were we to do with it? Even though I'd communicated that as part of the investment pitch, I still had to put the rubber to the road.'

This is day one

Now you have a good understanding of what investors look for and the mistakes start-up founders often make and how to avoid them, but reading the book is only the beginning. There's a huge amount of work required to get all six steps of the Investor Ready Roadmap right. Don't wait until you are about to go out pitching to work on everything you've learned in the book; use today as day one and continue on from here, every day. Lots of the things we've discussed in the book may take you time to put in place or create, so the sooner you start, the better.

Trying to get investment for your company is tough and can feel like an intimidating process, but if you've followed all the advice in the book, then you will have dramatically increased your chances of being successful and can feel confident with what you are putting in front of investors. As your company grows and changes, so you will need to refine some of your proposition and reiterate your documents and your pitch. Always come back to the six-step Investor Ready Roadmap to help you check you have everything covered.

You don't need to face this mammoth task alone. At the very least, find a mentor with some experience in this area who can help you as you prepare, and if you have funds available, outsource what you can of the research and document preparation.

A last request

At Spark! we're really passionate about supporting innovation in the UK. In fact, it's one of the UN Sustainable Development Goals that we actively support, so we want to see as many start-ups as possible succeed. Please pass on what you've learned from this book, or recommend it to other start-up founders so that they too can increase their chance of successfully winning investment.

And that's it! You've made it all the way through the process.

Acknowledgements

Writing a book, much like raising a child, takes a whole village. Without all the people I'd like to mention here, this book would never have made it to print. I am forever indebted to you all.

Thank you to my husband, Austin, for believing unfailingly in me, pouring me wine when it wasn't going well and picking up the slack through all the hours when I toiled on the book.

To Rafe, my miracle, who reminded me of the important things in life and why I shouldn't get stressed about writing a book.

To Daniel Priestley (CEO at Dent Global) for kick-starting me into realising my knowledge would work well as the content of a book.

To Jarmila Yu (amazing marketing strategist) and Mallika Paulraj (high net-worth investment advisor extraordinaire and best-connected woman in London) – thank you, ladies, you got me through the end, which was just as hard as the beginning and the middle.

A big thank you to all of the people who gave up time from their busy lives to be interviewed for this book:

Investors:

- Chris Adelsbach, UK Angel Investor of the Year 2018 and Techstars venture partner: www.techstars.com

- Russell Fisher, Head of Ventures, Nationwide Building Society: www.nbsventures.co.uk

- Jonathan Lerner, Managing Partner at Smedvig Capital: www.smedvigcapital.com

- Dan Bowyer, Co-Founder at SuperSeed: www.superseed.com

- Nic Brisbourne, Managing Partner at Forward Partners: www.forwardpartners.com

- Georgie Hazell, Head of Engagement at Augmentum plc: www.augmentum.vc

Industry experts:

- Luke Lang, Co-Founder of Crowdcube: www.crowdcube.com

- Samit Patel, Founder of Joopio Product marketing Agency https://joopio.com

- Ed Stephens, Head of Brokerage at the UK Angel Investment Network: www.angelinvestmentnetwork.co.uk

- Elle Berrett, a solicitor from Fusion Law who specialises in start-ups and scale-ups: www.fusionconsult.co.uk/fusion-law-services

- David Horne, Founder of Add Then Multiply, portfolio CFO and author: www.addthenmultiply.com

- Shaun Hyland, Reach Commercial Finance: www.reachcf.co.uk

Start-ups:

- Mark Abbott, CCO at Supermoney: www.supermoney.com

- Deborah Lygonis, Founder at Friendbase: www.friendbase.com

- Vanessa Tierney, Co-Founder at Abodoo: www.abodoo.com

- Heather McDonald, Founder at WooHa Brewing: www.woohabrewing.com

- Emma Ash, Co-Founder at YoungPlanet: www.youngplanet.com

- James White, sales mentor: www.jameswhite. business

- Joe Sillett, Co-Founder of The Funky Appliance Company: www.funkyappliance.com

- Rick Rowan, Founder of NuroKor BioElectronics: www.nurokor.co.uk

These fantastic people gave their own time, for free, to read and critique my book, and their help was invaluable:

- Adrian Cudby, author of *Commercial Lending: Principles and practice*: www.linkedin.com/in/ adrian-cudby-19ba096

- Owen Williams at 6 Red Squares: www.6rs.co.uk

- John Auckland at TribeFirst: www.tribefirst.co.uk

- Adina Luca at Profitable Insights: www.linkedin. com/in/adina-luca-44ba194

- Mark Abbott at Supermoney: www.supermoney. com

- James Adeleke at Generation Success: www. generation-success.com, an organisation I'm also proud to be a Non-Executive Director for

- Ceylan Boyce at the Academy for
  Women Entrepreneurs:
  www.academyforwomenentrepreneurs.com

And finally, thank you to Rethink Press for editing and publishing my book with care and professionalism.

The Author

Julie Barber is CEO of Spark! Consulting. Spark! works with large corporates who need to be more innovative and start-ups, scale-ups and SMEs to prepare them for raising investment and to support them on their further growth journey.

Julie spent twenty years in large corporate financial services before starting Spark!, focusing on innovation, corporate strategy and transformation, which included gaining more than £20 million in investment from corporate boards. With experience at large financial corporates like KPMG and HSBC, and quasi-regulators like the Financial Services Compensation

Scheme, she has implemented innovation practices and people, process and technology change across a quarter of a million user bases and up to 140 countries, with programmes she's led shortlisted for the UK IT Industry Awards.

With extensive experience on the 'buy' side when it comes to start-up investment and corporate sales, Julie has the inside track on what investors are looking for, and now brings that knowledge to bear in her work with start-ups. She believes that start-ups and large corporates can learn huge amounts from each other and consequently continues to work with both.

Julie is passionate about supporting UK innovation and attracting as much investment capital as possible to UK shores. She is also an active supporter of charities supporting women escaping domestic abuse, and Spark! donates 2% of its turnover annually to support these charities.

Feel free to get in contact via Julie's website, the Spark website or via social media.

⊕ https://juliebarber.co.uk

⊕ www.spark-consulting.co.uk

in www.linkedin.com/in/julieabarber

f www.facebook.com/JulieBarberSpark

Made in the USA
Las Vegas, NV
01 February 2022

42770739R10164